multiply

multiply

disciples making disciples

francis chan

with mark beuving

foreword by **david platt**

David C Cook

transforming lives together

MULTIPLY
Published by David C Cook
4050 Lee Vance View
Colorado Springs, CO 80918 U.S.A.

David C Cook Distribution Canada
55 Woodslee Avenue, Paris, Ontario, Canada N3L 3E5

David C Cook U.K., Kingsway Communications
Eastbourne, East Sussex BN23 6NT, England

The graphic circle C logo is a registered trademark of David C Cook.

The website addresses recommended throughout this book are offered as a
resource to you. These websites are not intended in any way to be or imply an
endorsement on the part of David C Cook, nor do we vouch for their content.

Unless otherwise noted, all Scripture quotations are taken from The Holy Bible,
English Standard Version® (ESV®), copyright © 2001 by Crossway, a publishing
ministry of Good News Publishers. Used by permission. All rights reserved.
The author has added italics to Scripture quotations for emphasis.

LCCN 2012947831
ISBN 978-0-7814-0824-0
eISBN 978-1-4347-0586-0

© 2012 Francis Chan, Mark Beuving

The Team: Don Pape, Amy Konyndyk, Renada Arens, Karen Athen
Cover Design: Jim Elliston, Nick Lee

Printed in the United States of America
First Mass Market Edition 2012

3 4 5 6 7 8 9 10

111612

Contents

Part V: Understanding the New Testament

Where Do We Go from Here?

Foreword

From the beginning of Christianity, the natural overflow of being a disciple of Jesus has always been to make disciples of Jesus. "Follow me," Jesus said, "and I will make you fishers of men" (Matt. 4:19). This was a promise: Jesus would take His disciples and turn them into disciple makers. And this was a command: He called each of His disciples to go and make disciples of all nations, baptizing them and teaching them to obey Him (Matt. 28:19–20). From the start, God's design has been for every single disciple of Jesus to make disciples who make disciples who make disciples until the gospel spreads to all peoples.

Yet we have subtly and tragically taken this costly command of Christ to go, baptize, and teach all nations and mutated it into a comfortable call for Christians to come, be baptized, and listen in one location. If you were to ask individual Christians today what it means to make disciples, you would likely get jumbled thoughts, ambiguous answers, and probably even some blank stares. In all our activity as Christians and with all our resources in the church, we are in danger of practically ignoring the commission of Christ. We view evangelism as a dreaded topic, we reduce discipleship to a canned program, and so many in the church end up sidelined in a spectator mentality that delegates disciple making to pastors and professionals, ministers and missionaries.

But this is not the way it's supposed to be. Jesus has invited all of us to be a part of His plan. He has designed all of His people to know His joy as we share His love, spread His Word, and multiply His life among all of the peoples of the earth. This is the grand purpose for which we were created: to enjoy the grace of Christ as we spread the gospel of Christ from wherever we live to the ends of the earth. And this purpose is worth giving our lives to seeing it accomplished. It's worth it for billions of people who do not yet know the mercy and majesty of God in Christ. And it's worth it for you and me, because we were made to be disciples who make disciples until the day when we see the face of the One we follow, and together with all nations we experience His satisfaction for all of eternity.

This is the heart behind the material you hold in your hand. When Francis Chan and I first met, our hearts immediately reso-nated around a shared passion for making disciples. We have a lot to learn, but we eagerly want to make disciples in our lives, and we zealously long to see every member of the church mobilized to make disciples through their lives. This material is part of the product of that passion. Francis and Mark have provided a simple, practical, biblical, helpful, and personal tool for disciples of Jesus who want to make disciples of Jesus. I pray that it will be used in God's mercy to fuel the multiplication of the love and life of Christ literally all over the world ultimately for the glory of God's name.

David Platt

How to Use the Material

After Jesus rose from the grave, He left His followers with a simple command: "Go into all the world and make disciples" (see Matt. 28:19). The church should be known for this. If we are going to call ourselves followers of Jesus Christ, we should be making disciples.

But most Christians today are not known for making disciples. We have developed a culture where a minister ministers and the rest of us sit back and enjoy "church" from a comfortable distance. This is not what God intends for His church. Every Christian is called by God to minister. You are called to make disciples.

Multiply is designed as a simple resource that you can use to begin making disciples. Our prayer is that it will give you the confidence you need to step out in faith and disciple the people whom God has placed in your life.

Using This Material

The goals of the *Multiply* material are to help you understand the Scripture and to give you the tools to disciple others in this process.

We have a responsibility to grow in our love and service to God and others. This is what it means to be the church. We are not merely responsible for our own spiritual well-being; we are called to minister to the people around us, teaching them to obey all the things that Jesus commands.

For this reason, there are two guidelines we ask you to follow when using this material. Obviously, we can't force you to use this curriculum in a specific way, but it's good for you to know the heart behind *Multiply*.

1. Teach what you learn. This material is not meant to be read, but to be taught. There are plenty of other Bible studies you can do if you just want to absorb more information. The emphasis of *Multiply* is to get you in the habit of passing on the knowledge you gain.
2. Share life, not just information. The *Multiply* process is meant to be highly relational. True discipleship involves deep relationships. Jesus didn't simply lead a weekly Bible study. He lived life with His disciples and taught through actions as well as words. While this requires a much deeper commitment, it is the only way to truly make disciples.

God wants us to live, serve, and process truth in the context of a community. You will encounter many difficult questions and life-changing truths in the weeks ahead. Working together with other people will be invaluable as you seek to sort out what the Bible is saying and how God wants that truth to play out in your life.

Discipleship by definition requires a leader and followers. This material is designed for a leader and a disciple to work through together. This doesn't mean that the leader needs to be old and completely mature, or that the disciple needs to be a full-fledged novice. We're all at varying stages of maturity, and we all need the people around us to help guide us toward Christlikeness. But ideally, you will either lead another person through this material or be guided through it by a more mature Christian. The goal is that once you've walked through the material, you can turn around and guide someone else through it. In fact, you are encouraged to guide others as you are learning. Don't wait until you have completed it all before teaching others what you learn.

God wants us to be talking about Him all throughout the week. Discipleship is all about living life together rather than just one structured meeting per week. However, it's shocking how quickly time gets away from us, so it's good to establish at least one regular meeting time each week. Without a little bit of structure, our good intentions often don't result in action. At the core of the *Multiply* material are weekly sessions, which involve study guides and videos.

Weekly Study Guide

Every week you will work through a session of the study guide. These study guides will help you reflect on biblical truths and how those truths should shape your life. Some of the sessions focus on key concepts related to discipleship—what it means to be a disciple, how the Bible is meant to be studied, how we help the people around us live in obedience to Jesus, etc. Other sessions focus on important biblical concepts and major developments in the biblical storyline—creation, the fall, God's covenant with Abraham, the life and death of Jesus Christ, etc. In each of these sessions you will read sections of Scripture and think through the truths presented and their implications for your life and ministry. The goal is to understand what the Bible is saying and allow that truth to transform your thought process and lifestyle.

Each study-guide session includes a number of questions that will challenge you to think about the material you have covered. These questions can also be used to structure the time you spend meeting with your disciple(s)/discipler(s). When you work through the study guide on your own, you can read through the material and answer the questions. When you meet with your partner(s), however, you can simply jump from one question to the next, sharing your answers and addressing any other thoughts or questions your study raised. If you are taking someone else (or a small group) through this material, don't feel any pressure to know more than everyone else. Knowledge isn't the point. Instead, start a discussion on the material in the study guides (this is where the questions come in handy). We all "know" things that have no practical bearing on our lives, so the more you can make your discussion practical and applicational, the better.

Each of these weekly sessions is available for free download at multiplymovement.com so that you can take as many people through this material as possible without putting a financial strain on anyone.

Weekly Video

Each session also includes a video (roughly five minutes long). You can find these videos at multiplymovement.com. The videos are designed for the leaders. If you are guiding another person through the material, the videos will coach you on how to truly "disciple" someone through these truths. Ideally, you will first work through the study guide session and answer all the questions. You may want to write in your book or use a separate notebook. Then you will watch the video and take notes on how you want to guide your disciple(s) through the session. (It shouldn't be problematic if your disciple wants to watch the videos as well, but the videos are directed toward the leaders.)

Structuring Your Weekly Meetings

Each person will be approaching this material from a unique position and in a unique setting. So structure your weekly meetings according to your specific needs and restraints. If you are leading your meetings, be sure to spend time talking through the material you covered for that week. The questions in the study guide sessions are designed to guide your discussion, but you may come up with a number of other important issues to address.

As important as covering the material is, make sure that you don't stop there. God's Word is meant to change our lives; James says that if all we do is hear the Word but never put it into practice, then we are deceiving ourselves (James 1:22). In many ways, it's better to not know His commands than to know and ignore them. Don't fall into the trap of studying the Bible without doing what it says. Take

time to share prayer requests, discuss personal sins and struggles, and
hold each other accountable to living out the truth of God's Word.

What You're Working Toward

Being a disciple of Jesus Christ means that we learn from Him, fellowship with Him, and obey everything He commands us. We study
the Bible to learn about who God is, who we are, and what God is
doing in our world. The Bible compels us to join God in what He
is doing in and around us. Studying the Bible is important, but the
goal is never knowledge for the sake of knowledge.

As you work through this material, you should be looking to
change. Being a disciple of Jesus means that we are being transformed into His image. God wants to change us so much that it
intrigues others. This gives us the opportunity to tell them about
the God who is transforming us. Teaching others about Christ is
essential to being one of Jesus's disciples. As we teach others to love
and obey Jesus, we are fulfilling His command to make disciples.
Your goal should be to train up other followers of Jesus who are even
more committed, talented, and equipped than you are. Whether you
guide others through this material or use some other means to teach
them to be followers of Jesus, make it your goal to spend your life
raising up followers who will give everything for the glory of God.

1: What Is a Disciple?

Two thousand years ago, Jesus walked up to a handful of men and said, "Follow me."

Imagine being one of those original disciples. They were ordinary people like you and me. They had jobs, families, hobbies, and social lives. As they went about their business on the day Jesus called them, none of them would have expected his life to change so quickly and completely.

The disciples could not have fully understood what they were getting into when they responded to Jesus's call. Whatever expectations or doubts, whatever curiosity, excitement, or uncertainty they felt, nothing could have prepared them for what lay ahead. Everything about Jesus—His teaching, compassion, and wisdom; His life, death, and resurrection; His power, authority, and calling— would shape every aspect of the rest of their lives.

In only a few years, these simple men were standing before some of the most powerful rulers on earth and being accused of "turn[ing] the world upside down" (Acts 17:6). What began as simple obedience to the call of Jesus ended up changing their lives, and ultimately, the world.

What Is a Disciple?

What does it mean to be a disciple of Jesus Christ? As you will discover, the answer is fairly simple, but it changes your life completely.

The word *disciple* refers to a student or apprentice. Disciples in Jesus's day would follow their rabbi (which means teacher) wherever he went, learning from the rabbi's teaching and being trained to do as the rabbi did. Basically, a disciple is a follower, but only if we take the term *follower* literally. Becoming a disciple of Jesus is as simple as obeying His call to follow.

When Jesus called His first disciples, they may not have understood where Jesus would take them or the impact it would have on their lives, but they knew what it meant to follow. They took Jesus's call literally and began going everywhere He went and doing everything He did.

It's impossible to be a disciple or a follower of someone and not end up like that person. Jesus said, "A disciple is not above his teacher, but everyone when he is fully trained will be like his teacher" (Luke 6:40). That's the whole point of being a disciple of Jesus: we imitate Him, carry on His ministry, and become like Him in the process.

Yet somehow many have come to believe that a person can be a "Christian" without being like Christ. A "follower" who doesn't follow. How does that make any sense? Many people in the church have decided to take on the *name* of Christ and nothing else. This would be like Jesus walking up to those first disciples and saying, "Hey, would you guys mind identifying yourselves with Me in some way? Don't worry, I don't actually care if you do anything I do or change your lifestyle at all. I'm just looking for people who are willing to say they believe in Me and call themselves Christians." Seriously?

No one can really believe that this is all it means to be a Christian. But then why do so many people live this way? It appears that we've lost sight of what it means to be a follower of Jesus. The concept of being a disciple isn't difficult to understand, but it affects everything.

1. *Up to this point in your life, would you call yourself a follower of Jesus Christ? Why do you say that? Do you see evidence of your faith as described in Luke 6:40?*

How Do I Become a Disciple?

To understand how to become a disciple of Jesus Christ, it makes most sense to start where Jesus started. While it is true that He said to the disciples, "Follow me, and I will make you fishers of men" (Matt. 4:19), the Bible records one message He proclaimed before that. In Matthew 4:17, Jesus said, "Repent, for the kingdom of heaven is at hand."

Try taking this phrase literally. If someone warned you to be prepared because a king and his army were coming, what would you do? You would make sure you were ready to face him. If you weren't prepared to fight this king, then you would do whatever it took to make peace with him.

The word *repent* means "to turn." It has the idea of changing directions and heading the opposite way. It involves action. In this context, Jesus was telling people to prepare themselves—to change whatever needed to be changed—because God's kingdom (the kingdom of heaven) was approaching.

So how do we prepare to face this heavenly kingdom? How do we make sure we are at peace with this coming King?

Jesus says we need to repent. This implies that we all need to turn from the way we are currently thinking and living. Romans 3:23 explains that "all have sinned and fall short of the glory of God." Every person reading this sentence has done things that are evil and offensive to this King. Romans later explains that "the wages of sin is death" (Rom. 6:23). Because of our sin, which is an offense to God, we should expect death. But then comes an amazing truth.

"But God shows his love for us in that while we were still sinners, Christ died for us" (Rom. 5:8). The death penalty we should have faced from this King was actually paid for by someone else. The King's Son, Jesus Christ![1]

---

1   These simple truths will be unpacked in far greater detail in Parts III and IV: "Understanding the Old Testament" and "Understanding the New Testament." The full significance of these truths will be explained then, but the truths themselves are important to understand from the outset.

The Scriptures then say, "If you confess with your mouth that Jesus is Lord and believe in your heart that God raised him from the dead, you will be saved" (Rom. 10:9). We are saved by the grace of God through faith in Jesus Christ. It is all about who Jesus is and what He has done. Part of our repentance is to turn from believing that there's anything we can do to save ourselves—for everything was accomplished by Jesus Christ.

The thought that someone else has paid for our crimes is strange to most of us because it defies our natural way of thinking. And the idea that we need to trust in another person's sacrifice on our behalf is even more foreign. But understand that while it is strange to us, it is consistent with God's actions throughout the Scriptures.

We get a picture of this when we read the book of Exodus. In this story, Moses warned Pharaoh repeatedly about what God would do if he did not repent. It climaxed when God said He would bring death to the firstborn of every household if they did not repent. Meanwhile, He told His people that if they put the blood of a lamb over their doorposts, His angel would pass over their homes and not kill the firstborn of that house. So even in the story of the exodus, we see that people had to trust in the blood of a lamb to save them— and this was the *only* way they could be saved.

2. *Read Ephesians 2 carefully and take some time to consider the truths it presents. Do you trust in the death of Christ for your salvation? Do you ever struggle with believing you need to do something to save yourself?*

The Lord of Grace

Salvation is all about the grace of God. There is absolutely nothing that you can do to save yourself or earn God's favor. Paul said, "By grace you have been saved through faith. And this is not your own doing; it is the gift of God, not a result of works, so that no one may boast" (Eph. 2:8–9). No one can brag about his or her good deeds because our works cannot save us. Salvation comes through the grace of God as we place our faith in Jesus Christ. All salvation requires is faith: Do you believe that Jesus is who He says He is?

But keep in mind that while this is simple, it's not easy. Faith in Jesus Christ means believing that He is Lord (according to Rom. 10:9). Have you ever thought about what that word *Lord* means? We sometimes think of it as another name for God, but it's actually a title. It refers to a master, owner, or a person who is in a position of authority. So take a minute to think this through: Do you really believe that Jesus is your master? Do you believe that He is your owner—that you actually belong to Him?

Paul is so bold as to tell us: "You are not your own, for you were bought with a price. So glorify God in your body" (1 Cor. 6:19–20). The same Lord who by His grace set us free from sin and death now owns us. We belong to Him, and He calls us to live in obedience to His rule.

The problem is, many in the church want to "confess that Jesus is Lord," yet they don't believe that He is their master. Do you see the obvious contradiction in this? The call to be a disciple of Jesus Christ is open to everyone, but we don't get to write our own job description. If Jesus is Lord, then He sets the agenda. If Jesus Christ is Lord, then your life belongs to Him. He has a plan, agenda, and calling for you. You don't get to tell Him what you'll be doing today or for the rest of your life.

3. *Evaluate your approach to following Jesus. Would you say that you view Jesus as your Lord, Master, and Owner? Why or why not?*

It All Comes Down to Love

But don't get the impression that following Jesus is all about joyless sacrifice. More than anything else, following Jesus boils down to two commands, which He said were the most important commandments in the Old Testament Law:

> You shall love the Lord your God with all your heart
> and with all your soul and with all your mind. This
> is the great and first commandment. And a second
> is like it: You shall love your neighbor as yourself.
> On these two commandments depend all the Law
> and the Prophets. (Matt. 22:37–40)

It all comes down to love. Peter expressed it well for people like us, who didn't see Jesus on earth but follow Him nonetheless: "Though you have not seen him, *you love him.* Though you do not now see him, *you believe in him and rejoice with joy that is inexpressible and filled with glory*" (1 Pet. 1:8).

Following Jesus is not about diligently keeping a set of rules or conjuring up the moral fortitude to lead good lives. It's about loving God and enjoying Him.

But lest we think that we can love God and live any way we want to, Jesus told us very clearly, "If you love me, you will keep my commandments" (John 14:15). The love for God in the first commandment is made practical in the love for our neighbors in the second commandment. John actually told us that if we don't love the people that we can see around us, then we don't love God, whom we can't see (1 John 4:20).

True love is all about sacrifice for the sake of the ones you love: "By this we know love, that he laid down his life for us, and we ought to lay down our lives for the brothers" (1 John 3:16). When we understand love in this light, it's not difficult to understand that love for God and obedience to Jesus Christ cannot be separated. God's love changes us from the inside out and redefines every aspect of our lives.

4. *As you look at your life, how would you say that your love for God is shown in your actions? (If you're having trouble coming up with an answer, take some time to think through some changes you may need to make in your lifestyle.)*

Count the Cost

As you work your way through this material, you will be challenged to consider what it means to be a follower of Jesus. You will think through what the Bible teaches and its implications for the way you live your life today. Everything you study will be for the purpose of applying it to your life and teaching other people to do the same. But before you set out to teach other people to be disciples of Jesus, you need to examine your heart and make sure you are a disciple.

Read the following words from Jesus slowly and carefully. Understand that Jesus is speaking these words to you. Think about what Jesus is saying and how it should affect the way you approach this material and your relationship with Him. After you have read this section, use the questions below to help you count the cost of following Jesus.

> Now great crowds accompanied him, and he turned and said to them, "If anyone comes to me and does not hate his own father and mother and wife and children and brothers and sisters, yes, and even his own life, he cannot be my disciple. Whoever does not bear his own cross and come after me cannot be my disciple. For which of you, desiring to build a tower, does not first sit down and count the cost, whether he has enough to complete it? Otherwise, when he has laid a foundation and is not able to finish, all who see it begin to mock him, saying, 'This man began to build and was not able to finish.' Or what king, going out to encounter another king in

war, will not sit down first and deliberate whether he is able with ten thousand to meet him who comes against him with twenty thousand? And if not, while the other is yet a great way off, he sends a delegation and asks for terms of peace. So therefore, any one of you who does not renounce all that he has cannot be my disciple." (Luke 14:25–33)

5. *If you choose to obey Jesus's call to follow, what might it cost you? (Avoid being vague. If following Jesus would cost you specific possessions, comforts, or relationships, list them below.)*

6. *What might hold you back from following Jesus at this point? Are you willing to let go of these things if necessary?*

7. *Before you end this session, spend some time in prayer. Ask God to work in your heart and prepare you for what is ahead. You don't need to have all the answers or know specifically how God will use you. He simply calls you to follow wherever He might lead. As you pray, be honest about your doubts, hesitations, and fears. Ask Him to give you the strength to proceed and follow Him no matter what the cost. In other words, place your faith in Him.*

 Watch the video for this session at multiplymovement.com.

2: The Command to Make Disciples

Imagine your reaction if someone came back from the dead to speak to you. Seriously, try to imagine that right now. What would you feel? How intensely would you listen? How seriously would you take his or her words?

Think about what this must have been like for the disciples. They were working their everyday jobs when a mysterious teacher asked them to follow Him. As they followed, they saw Him challenge religious leaders, embrace sinners, heal the sick, and even raise the dead. They knew that He was not an ordinary man. At various times and to varying degrees, people saw Him as the Messiah who would bring salvation for God's people. But He never quite fit anyone's expectations of what the Messiah would do or say.

The disciples walked beside Jesus through all of this. They watched as the blind were given sight. They heard Jesus forgive the hopelessly unrighteous and restore the lives of the broken. They helped pass out bread and fish as Jesus miraculously fed huge crowds. The disciples seem to have been more aware of Jesus's true identity at some points than at others, but they followed Him until the end, believing that He was the one who would restore the fortunes of God's people.

And then He died. Just like that. It was over. It seemed that Jesus could do absolutely anything, that He had power over sickness, death, every person, and every thing. By this power, Jesus was bringing the healing and redemption that the world so desperately needed. But the disciples' hopes of a better world died as Jesus was nailed to a Roman cross.

And so the disciples spent three days in confusion and disillusionment. Everything they had hoped for was gone. Perhaps they had wasted their time following this mysterious person for three years.

Then it happened. He came back from the dead! When Jesus reappeared on the third day, all of their hope came rushing back! Now there could be no doubt! Now that Jesus had conquered even sin and death, He would certainly fix this broken world. Jesus would accomplish what everyone was longing to see. There could be no stopping Him.

Once again, He surprised everyone. Instead of telling them that He would immediately transform the earth, Jesus gave His disciples one final command and ascended into heaven. Just like that, out of nowhere. What was the command? Essentially, He told them it was their job to finish what He started. They were to take the message that Jesus declared and exemplified in and around Jerusalem and spread that message to the very ends of the earth:

All authority in heaven and on earth has been given to me. Go therefore and make disciples of all nations, baptizing them in the name of the Father and of the Son and of the Holy Spirit, teaching them to observe all that I have commanded you. And behold, I am with you always, to the end of the age. (Matt. 28:18–20)

1. *Stop for a minute and read Matthew 28. Try to place yourself in the disciples' shoes as they witnessed these things and heard these words from Jesus. How do you think you would have reacted?*

The Great Commission and the Church

So what comes to your mind when you think about Jesus's command to make disciples of all nations? Many read these words as if they were meant to inspire pastors or missionaries on their way out to the mission field. But have you ever considered that maybe Jesus's command is meant for *you*?

As we read the rest of the New Testament, we see God's people working together in obedience to Jesus's command. They reached out to the people around them, calling them to obediently follow Jesus. The disciples went about making disciples, teaching them to obey everything that Jesus had commanded and baptizing them. Some of them even moved to different areas or traveled around so that they could tell more people. They took Jesus's words seriously—and literally.

Reading through the New Testament, it's not surprising to read that Jesus's followers were focused on making disciples—it makes sense in light of Jesus's ministry and the Great Commission. The surprise comes when we look at our churches today in light of Jesus's command to make disciples.

Why is it that we see so little disciple making taking place in the church today? Do we really believe that Jesus told His early followers to make disciples but wants the twenty-first-century church to do something different? None of us would claim to believe this, but somehow we have created a church culture where the paid ministers do the "ministry," and the rest of us show up, put some money in the plate, and leave feeling inspired or "fed." We have moved so far away from Jesus's command that many Christians don't have a frame of reference for what disciple making looks like.

2. *Assess your church experience in light of Jesus's command to make disciples. Would you say that your church is characterized by disciple making? Why or why not?*

More Than a Program

So what does disciple making look like? We have to be careful about how we answer this question. For some of us, our church experience has been so focused on programs that we immediately think about Jesus's command to make disciples in programmatic terms. We expect our church leaders to create some sort of disciple-maker campaign where we sign up, commit to participating for a few months, and then get to cross the Great Commission off our list. But making disciples is far more than a program. It is the mission of our lives. It defines us. A disciple is a disciple maker.

So what does this look like? The Great Commission uses three phrases to describe what disciple making entails: go, baptize people, and teach them to obey everything Jesus commanded. Simple, right? It's incredibly simple in the sense that it doesn't require a degree, an ordination process, or some sort of hierarchical status. It's as simple as going to people, encouraging them to follow Jesus (this is what baptism is all about), and then teaching them to obey Jesus's commands (which we find in the Bible). The concept itself is not very difficult.

But the simplest things to understand are often the most difficult to put into practice. Let's start with baptism. In your church setting, baptism may not seem like that big of a deal. Maybe that's why so many Christians today have never been baptized. But in the early days of the church, baptism was huge. Baptism was an unmistakable act that marked a person as a follower of Jesus Christ. As Jesus died and was buried in the earth, so a Christian is plunged beneath the surface of the water. As Jesus emerged from the tomb in a resurrected body, so a Christian comes out of the waters of baptism as a new creation.

When first-century Christians took this step of identifying themselves with the death and resurrection of Jesus, they were publicly declaring their allegiance to Christ. This immediately marked them for martyrdom—all of the hostility that the world felt toward Jesus would now be directed at them. Baptism was a declaration that a person's life, identity, and priorities were centered on Jesus and His mission. Depending on where you live in the world, you may not see the same reaction to your choice to be baptized, but that act of identifying with Christ is essential, no matter where you live.

3. *Have you identified yourself with Jesus through being baptized? If so, why do you think this was an important step for you to take? If not, what is holding you back from being baptized?*

Just as baptism is more significant than we might have thought, so teaching people to obey Jesus's commands is an enormous task. Realistically, this will require a lifetime of devotion to studying the Scriptures and investing in the people around us. Neither of these things is easy, nor can they be checked off of a list. We are never really "done." We continually devote ourselves to studying the Scriptures so that we can learn with ever-greater depth and clarity what God wants us to know, practice, and pass on. We continually invest in the people around us, teaching them and walking with them through life's joys and trials.

We never "finish" the discipleship process. It's much like raising a child: though there comes a day when she is ready to be on her own, the relationship doesn't end. The friendship continues, and there will always be times when guidance and encouragement are still needed. In addition to that, God continually brings new people into our path, giving us fresh opportunities to start the discipleship process all over again.

Following Jesus by making disciples isn't difficult to understand, but it can be very costly. Jesus's teachings are often difficult to stomach. By sharing His teachings, we are often rejected along with His message. Jesus said:

> If the world hates you, know that it has hated me before it hated you. If you were of the world, the world would love you as its own; but because you are not of the world, but I chose you out of the world, therefore the world hates you. Remember the word that I said to you: "A servant is not greater than his master." If they persecuted me, they will also persecute you. If they kept my word, they will also keep yours. (John 15:18–20)

It's easy enough to understand, but it can be extremely costly.

4. *Would you say that you're ready to commit yourself to studying the Scriptures and investing in the people around you? Why or why not?*

Equipped to Do the Work of Ministry

Unfortunately, disciple making has become the exclusive domain of pastors (and missionaries). Salesmen sell, insurance agents insure, and ministers minister. At least, that's the way it works in most of our churches.

While it's true that the pastors, elders, and apostles in the New Testament made disciples, we can't overlook the fact that discipleship was everyone's job. The members of the early church took their responsibility to make disciples very seriously. To them, the church wasn't a corporation run by a CEO. Rather, they compared the church to a body that functions properly only when every member is doing its part.

Paul explained the function of the church in Ephesians 4:11–16:

> He gave the apostles, the prophets, the evangelists, the shepherds and teachers, *to equip the saints for the work of ministry*, for building up the body of Christ … we are to grow up in every way into him who is the head, into Christ, from whom *the whole body, joined and held together by every joint with which it is equipped, when each part is working properly*, makes the body grow so that it builds itself up in love.

Paul saw the church as a community of redeemed people in which each person is actively involved in doing the work of ministry. The pastor is not the minister—at least not in the way we typically think of a minister. The pastor is the equipper, and every member of the church is a minister.

The implications are huge. Don't think of this as merely a theological issue. See yourself in this passage. Paul said that *your* job is to do the work of ministry! Jesus commanded *you* to make disciples!

Most Christians can give a number of reasons why they cannot or should not disciple other people: "I don't feel called to minister." "I just have too much on my plate right now; I don't have time to invest in other people." "I don't know enough." "I have too many issues of my own. I'll start once I get my life in order."

As convincing as these excuses may seem to us, Jesus's commands don't come with exception clauses. He doesn't tell us to follow *unless* we're busy. He doesn't call us to love our neighbors *unless* we don't feel prepared. In fact, if you read Luke 9:57–62, you'll see several individuals who gave excuses for why they couldn't follow Jesus at the time. Read the passage and take note of how Jesus responded to them. It may surprise you.

God made you the way you are; He has provided and will continue to provide you with everything you need to accomplish the task. Jesus commands you to look at the people around you and start making them into disciples. Obviously, only God can change people's hearts and make them want to become followers. We just have to be obedient in making the effort to teach them, even though we still have plenty to learn ourselves.

5. *What excuses tend to keep you from following Jesus's command to make disciples? What do you need to do in order to move past these excuses?*

Taking the First Step

Being a disciple maker means that you will begin to look at the people in your life differently. Every person in your life is created in the image of God, and Jesus commands every one of them to follow Him. God has placed these people in your life so that you will do everything you can to influence them. Following Jesus means that you will be teaching other people to follow Jesus.

Take some time to consider your first step toward disciple making. Whom has God placed in your life that you can teach to follow Jesus? Maybe God is laying someone on your heart you don't know very well. Your first step could be building a relationship with that person. Maybe it's someone you've known for years, and God is calling you to take that relationship to another level. God has placed you where you are, and the people around you are not there by accident. Keep in mind that the Great Commission calls us to every type of person, to those inside of the church as well as to those outside, to those who are like us and those who are very different. Everyone needs to understand who Jesus is and what it means to follow Him.

6. *Whom has God placed in your life right now that you can begin making into a disciple of Jesus Christ?*

Working Together to Make Disciples

God wants you to view the other Christians in your life as partners in ministry. God has not called you to make disciples in isolation; He has placed you in the context of a church body so that you can be encouraged and challenged by the people around you. And you are called to encourage and challenge them in return.

As you begin this study, think about how you will proceed. Are there Christians in your life you can study this material with? Are there mature believers you can approach with the questions that will inevitably arise? The goal is for you to think through this material and let these truths saturate your mind, heart, and lifestyle. But you'll get a lot more out of this if you have other people to talk with, be challenged by, and work together with. Human beings are simply not designed to function in isolation.

7. *Whom has God placed in your life for you to partner with in making disciples?*

8. *Spend some time praying that God will make you into a committed and effective disciple maker. Confess any feelings of unpreparedness and insecurity. Ask Him to empower you for the ministry He is*

calling you to. Ask Him to lead you to the right people to partner with and the right people to begin discipling.

 Watch the video for this session at multiplymovement.com.

3: The Heart of a Disciple Maker

Why do you want to make disciples?

Have you ever asked yourself that question? The answer is incredibly important.

As followers of Jesus Christ, we should be focused on making disciples. But if we don't do it with the right motives, we are wasting our time. Worse yet, we could be doing more harm than good. Ministering to other people has been a deadly trap for seemingly godly people throughout the ages. If God cared only about outward appearances and religious activities, then any effort toward ministry would please Him. But God tells us repeatedly that He cares more about the heart than the externals.

If God cared only about religious activities, then the Pharisees would have been heroes of the faith. They were continuously engaged in ministry: they vigorously pursued outward demonstrations of godliness; they made sure the people around them kept themselves holy, and they diligently taught the law of God. And yet the Gospels present the Pharisees as villains. Jesus's harshest words were reserved for these religious overachievers:

> This people honors me with their lips,
>   but their heart is far from me;
> in vain do they worship me,
>   teaching as doctrines the commandments of
>   men. (Matt. 15:8–9)

The Pharisees devoted their whole lives to religious activity. They must have seemed so impressive to the people around them. Yet Jesus came along and declared that it was all in vain! An important theme that runs throughout Scripture is this: "The LORD sees not as man sees: man looks on the outward appearance, but the LORD looks on the heart" (1 Sam. 16:7). Clearly, God wants us to pursue certain actions, but as we put God's commands into action, our motivation makes all the difference.

1. *Take a moment to examine your heart. In all honesty, why do you want to make disciples? Do you struggle with wanting your actions to be noticed by others?*

Teaching Is Dangerous

Ask yourself again: Why do you want to make disciples?

Maybe your decision to be a disciple maker has been reluctant. Perhaps the only reason you are still working through this material is because Jesus commands you to make disciples, and you don't want to be disobedient. You're not sure if you have much to offer, but you know you should let God use you however He desires.

Or maybe you've always seen yourself as a leader. You have a message that the church needs to hear, and you're ready to teach anyone who will listen. You don't need motivation; you just want to be better equipped.

For those of you who are reluctant, remember that God wants you to minister out of joy, not mere obligation. God wants us to enjoy the privilege and pleasure of ministering to others. He wants us to be cheerful when we give (2 Cor. 9:7), and He wants us to lead others willingly and eagerly:

> Shepherd the flock of God that is among you,
> exercising oversight, not under compulsion, but
> willingly, as God would have you; not for shameful
> gain, but eagerly. (1 Pet. 5:2)

For those who are eager to lead, remember that God wants us to be cautious as we lead. Remember that you will be teaching people about the Bible and guiding them into godly living. The Bible takes the role of a teacher very seriously, and so should we.

James gave us a terrifying warning about the power of the tongue. While we can speak truth and bring life to people, he warned that our words can also cause incredible damage. The tongue is untamable, James said, capable of diverting the direction of our lives, producing deadly poison, and "setting on fire the entire course of life" (James 3:6). Indeed, James even accused the tongue of being set on fire by hell!

If you look at your heart and find even a trace of desire for the glory and prestige that come through teaching and leading other people, take some time to let James's warning sink in. Think about what your tongue is capable of. As a disciple maker, you could make a huge impact for the kingdom of God. Or you could lead people horribly astray.

2. *Read James 3:1–12 and meditate on James's warning. How do these powerful words affect you? How might you need to adjust your approach to making disciples?*

Love Comes First

Paul added a challenge from a different angle. In the most beautiful terms, he said that gaining knowledge and power—even sacrificing our own bodies—is completely worthless apart from love:

> If I speak in the tongues of men and of angels, but have not love, I am a noisy gong or a clanging

cymbal. And if I have prophetic powers, and understand all mysteries and all knowledge, and if I have all
faith, so as to remove mountains, but have not love, I
am nothing. If I give away all I have, and if I deliver
up my body to be burned, but have not love, I gain
nothing. (1 Cor. 13:1–3)

The result of loveless ministry is serious: *I am a noisy gong or a clanging cymbal … I am nothing … I gain nothing.* In other words, even the most impressive and sacrificial actions are worthless if they are not empowered by love.

Are you the type of person who would teach someone without loving them? Don't be quick to answer. Many good pastors have confessed that they got so caught up in the busyness of ministry that they went through the motions without loving their people. Most of us have to work hard to keep love at the forefront.

What do you think and feel when you are in a group of people? Are you overly aware of the ones who are wealthy, attractive, or have something they can offer you? Do you worry about what people think of you? Or do you look for ways to love and opportunities to give? A sure sign of a loveless heart is seeing people as a means to your own ends—they listen to you, give you affirmation when you want it, stay out of your way when you don't, etc. Teaching other people with this type of mentality is bound to be sterile and unfruitful. According to Paul, every time we try to teach someone with this mentality, we can be sure that we have become nothing more than a clanging gong or resounding cymbal; we have made ourselves both annoying and irrelevant.

Fulfilling Jesus's command to make disciples is about more than having the right theology or well-developed teaching points. Remember that if you "understand all mysteries and all knowledge" yet don't have love, you are nothing. Earlier in the same letter, Paul said, "If anyone imagines that he knows something, he does not yet know as he ought to know. But if anyone loves God, he is known by God" (1 Cor. 8:2–3). It's not about what you know—or what you *think* you know—it's about love.

If you're not willing to make loving God and loving people your highest priority, then stop. Seriously, walk away until you've settled this one essential point. Lack of love is the unmistakable mark of death: "We know that we have passed out of death into life, because we love the brothers. Whoever does not love abides in death" (1 John 3:14).

Making disciples isn't about gathering pupils to listen to your teaching. The real focus is not on teaching people at all—the focus is on loving them. Jesus's call to make disciples includes teaching people to be obedient followers of Jesus, but the teaching isn't the end goal. Ultimately, it's all about being faithful to God's call to love the people around you. It's about loving those people enough to help them see their need to love and obey God. It's about bringing them to the Savior and allowing Him to set them free from the power of sin and death and transform them into loving followers of Jesus Christ. It's about glorifying God by obediently making disciples who will teach others to love and obey God.

So the question is, how much do you care about the people around you? When you stand in a crowd, interact with your family, or talk to people in your church, do you love them and long to see them glorify God in every aspect of their lives? Honestly assessing your heart and asking God to purify your motives need to become habits in your life.

3. *Up to this point, would you say that your desire to make disciples has been motivated by love? Why or why not?*

Take some time to consider your existing relationships—family, friends, coworkers, neighbors, etc. The way you think about and interact with the people that God has placed in your life can tell you a lot about your heart. Think about your relationships and ask yourself how well you love those around you. By assessing your current relationships, you should be able to identify areas you need to work on.

4. *Describe your love for the people God has placed in your life. What evidence can you point to that shows that you love the people around you?*

5. *In addition to praying fervently, what practical steps can you take to
    increase your love for people?*

Teaching by Example

One of the worst things you can do is teach truths that you are not
applying. We call this hypocrisy, and it's the most common criticism
of Christians in America. You could argue that it may be better not
to teach at all than to teach truth without applying it to your own
life. Jesus gave some harsh warnings toward the religious leaders who
were doing that very thing. He said:

> Do and observe whatever they [the scribes and
> Pharisees] tell you, but not the works they do. For
> they preach, but do not practice. They tie up heavy
> burdens, hard to bear, and lay them on people's
> shoulders, but they themselves are not willing to
> move them with their finger. They do all their deeds
> to be seen by others. (Matt. 23:3–5)

Hypocrisy has damaged many, so let's run far from it.

James also gave a strong warning against this type of thinking.
He said that if we hear the Word of God, but don't do what it
says, we are merely deceiving ourselves (James 1:22–25). He went

on to say that religion without practical action is worthless (vv. 26–27). Let's be realistic: a self-deceived teacher who practices worthless religion is probably not the best candidate for a disciple maker.

Maybe the clearest explanation of teaching by example can be found in the book of Hebrews: "Remember your leaders, those who spoke to you the word of God. Consider the outcome of their way of life, and imitate their faith" (Heb. 13:7). The author of Hebrews actually called us to consider—literally, "to examine carefully"—the outcome of a teacher's lifestyle. We can get so caught up in examining a person's doctrinal positions that we overlook his or her pattern of life. But this is essential because Hebrews calls us to imitate the faith of these people. If you are going to make disciples, you need to be putting your faith into practice so that the people around you can imitate your faith.

Because of this, being a disciple maker demands your entire life. The job description of a disciple maker is the same as that of a disciple of Jesus Christ. It requires everything. It means following Jesus in every aspect of your life, pursuing Him with a wholehearted devotion. If you're not ready to lay down your life for Christ's sake, then you're not ready to make disciples. It's that simple.

This doesn't mean that you need to be perfect before you start. Perfection is a lifelong process that won't end until eternity (see Phil. 1:6 and 3:12–14). But it does mean that you need to "count the cost" (see Luke 14:25–33) and allow God's truth to change your life. Making disciples is all about seeing people transformed by the power of God's Word. If you want to see that happen in others, you need to be experiencing such transformation yourself.

6. Would you say that your life is being transformed by the truth of God's Word? Why or why not?

7. What changes do you need to make in order to live the truths that you will be teaching other people?

8. The things you've been thinking through in this session are not easy to address—there are no "quick fixes" here. End your time with this session by praying that God will give you the proper motivation to make disciples, increase your love for Him and the people around you, and empower you to live out the truths that He has called you to teach to others.

Watch the video for this session at multiplymovement.com.

1: Life in the Church

Not every culture is individualistic. But in the Western world, we tend to look up to Lone Rangers. Our heroes are strong and self-sufficient, and they tend to walk alone. Very often, the Western church tends toward this type of individualism. We hear Jesus's call to take up our cross and follow Him, and we decide to follow no matter what anyone else says or does. Of course, this is the right response, but we need to be careful here. While *every individual* needs to obey Jesus's call to follow, we cannot follow Jesus *as individuals*. The proper context for every disciple maker is the church. It is impossible to make disciples aside from the church of Jesus Christ. Look at it from this perspective: the New Testament is full of commands to do this or that for "one another." Love one another, pray for one another, encourage one another, etc. So how can we teach people to "observe all that I have commanded" if they have no one to love, pray for, or encourage? It's impossible to "one another" yourself. It's impossible to follow Jesus alone. We can't claim to follow Jesus if we neglect the church He created, the church He died for, the church He entrusted His mission to.

In this session and the two following sessions, we will place disciple making squarely within the context of the church. This session will examine the way in which we are called to live together as the church. Teaching people to obey what Jesus commanded is a never-ending process that requires us to intertwine our lives with the Christians around us. As disciple makers, we will join together with other believers, help them overcome the sin that holds them back, and challenge them to grow into more effective disciple makers.

The next two sessions will focus on the call to reach out to the people in our local setting and to the rest of the world. In each case, our call is to make disciples, and we must learn to fulfill that calling through the God-ordained vehicle of the church.

Committing Your Life to the Church

First, let's make sure that we are not guilty of belittling God's church in any way. It's not a social club; it's not a building, and it's not an option. The church is life and death. The church is God's strategy for reaching our world. What we do inside the church matters. We tend to equate church life with events and programs. But these are not what make a church. Programs are helpful to the extent that they facilitate the life and mission of the church, but we can't equate well-attended events with the health of the church.

God cares about the way we love each other and the way we pursue His mission. The church is a group of redeemed people that live and serve together in such a way that their lives and communities are transformed. What matters is your interaction with the people God has placed in your life. If you are not connected with other Christians, serving and being served, challenging and being challenged, then you are not living as He desires, and the church is not functioning as He intended.

Throughout the Bible, we see pictures of the global church (which includes all followers of Jesus in all locations) and the local church (which includes particular followers of Jesus in a particular location). Out of 114 times that the "church" is mentioned in the New Testament, at least ninety of them refer to specific local gatherings of believers who have banded together for fellowship and mission. God intends for every follower of Jesus to be a part of such a gathering under the servant leadership of pastors who shepherd the church for the glory of God.

Despite the clear priority that the Bible puts on believers being part of a local church, many followers of Christ try to live the Christian life apart from serious, personal commitment to a local church. The reasons are many. We are self-reliant and self-sufficient, and the kind of mutual interdependence and even submission and accountability to others that the Bible talks about frightens us. We are often indecisive, hopping from one church to another looking for the "perfect place" and the "perfect people." Many of us have been hurt in the past by things that have happened to or around us in the church, and others of us simply don't see the importance of being specifically connected to a local church.

But the Bible says the local church is important. God has entrusted local churches with godly leaders who teach us His Word and care for our souls (Heb. 13:17; 1 Pet. 5:1–8; 1 Tim. 3:1–13;

5:17; Titus 1:5–9). God has united us together in local churches to keep one another from sinning and straying from Christ (Gal. 6:1–5; Matt. 18:15–20). God has commanded us to gather together in local assemblies where we preach God's Word, celebrate the Lord's Supper, baptize new believers, and pray for and encourage one another (Acts 2:42; Heb. 10:24–25). Then we scatter to care for believers and to share the gospel with unbelievers (Acts 2:43–47). Clearly, being a disciple and making disciples involves committing your life to a local church where you are joined together with other believers under biblical leadership to grow in the likeness of Christ and to express the love of Christ to the world around you.

1. *Why do you think the New Testament places such a priority on Christians being committed members (or parts) of local churches? How can this priority best be reflected in your life?*

2. *Read Ephesians 4:1–16. How should this passage affect the way you view your responsibility to other Christians in the church?*

Bearing One Another's Burdens

In Part I, we said that every Christian is a minister. Paul said that God gave pastors, teachers, and elders to the church so that they could teach the rest of us to minister. A pastor's job is not to do all of the ministry in a church, but to "equip the saints for the work of ministry, for building up the body of Christ" (Eph. 4:12).

So the question becomes: Whom should you be ministering to and how? Don't be overwhelmed by the task of ministering to others. It is just about faithfully serving the people God has placed in your life. Paul explained:

> Brothers, if anyone is caught in any transgression,
> you who are spiritual should restore him in a spirit
> of gentleness. Keep watch on yourself, lest you too
> be tempted. Bear one another's burdens, and so
> fulfill the law of Christ. (Gal. 6.1–2)

Ministry sounds intimidating until you develop a realistic view of what ministry is really about. Maybe you're not gifted to preach sermons, start a rehabilitation clinic, or lead a marriage retreat. But do you know people who struggle with sin? Do you know people who are carrying burdens? If so, then your first steps toward ministry are easy: help them.

We don't like getting involved in other people's problems. Our own problems are messy enough—why complicate things by taking on other people's junk? But the reason is simple: God calls us to help other people. He created us to function this way. Your problems are not just your problems—ultimately, they belong to the church body that God has placed you in. You are called to encourage, challenge, and help the other Christians in your life, and they are called to do the same for you. If you wait until all of your own issues are gone before helping others, it will never happen. This is a trap that millions have fallen into, not realizing that our own sanctification happens *as* we minister to others.

3. *Think about your unique setting and identify a few opportunities that God has given you to minister to the people around you. Have you taken advantage of these opportunities?*

4. *Take a few minutes to meditate on Galatians 6:1–2. What would it look like to help bear someone else's burden? Is there anyone in your life right now whom you should be helping in this way?*

Getting beneath the Surface

We have to be clear about what it means to help the people God has placed in our lives. We gravitate toward solutions that are quick and easy. When it comes to helping people, we often address the surface level of the problem but never get down to the heart of the matter. When someone is grieving, we might hand him a book that helped us in a difficult moment. But how many of us would take the time to really invest in his life? Would we listen on a consistent basis and offer help whenever we find a need that we are able to meet?

Or when we learn that a friend is struggling with sin, we are quick to explain why that sin is harmful and tell her we will pray for her (whether we follow through or not). But how many of us would take her struggle with sin so seriously that we would walk with her as she works through the issues involved?

It's not that Christians are uncaring. Very often, we really do want to help the people around us however we can, but we get so focused on finding a quick solution to the external behavior that we overlook the real problem. Here's an example. If a friend struggles with anger, we find out what makes him angry, and then keep him away from the things that provoke his anger (e.g., don't drive during rush hour, interact with your boss as little as possible, avoid talking politics). But changing the external situation doesn't change his heart. In reality, his anger is rooted in his heart, and that anger will find a way to express itself even if his circumstances change.

When Jesus's disciples started eating without going through the necessary cleansing rituals, the Pharisees accused them of defiling themselves. But Jesus's response calls us to look beyond the external to what is going on in the heart:

"Whatever goes into a person from outside cannot defile him, since it enters not his heart but his stomach, and is expelled?" (Thus he declared all foods clean.) And he said, "What comes out of a person is what defiles him. For from within, out of the heart of man, come evil thoughts, sexual immorality, theft, murder, adultery, coveting, wickedness, deceit, sensuality, envy, slander, pride, foolishness. All these evil things come from within, and they defile a person. (Mark 7:18–23)

Every struggle with sin that we could possibly encounter in our own lives or in the lives of the people around us are represented in the list Jesus offered here: evil thoughts, sexual immorality, theft, murder, adultery, coveting, wickedness, deceit, sensuality, envy, slander, pride, and foolishness. Jesus said that these things come from within. In other words, if we are trying to address these problems by regulating a person's circumstances or behavior, then we are wasting our time. These things come "out of the heart of man." Whatever help we can offer people who are struggling with sin has to be aimed at transforming hearts, not behavior.

5. *Why do you think we tend to focus on the external circumstances and behavior when we try to help people change?*

6. *Using your own words, try to explain why it is essential to get to the
    heart of the problem rather than merely addressing the circumstances
    and behavior.*

Transformed by the Gospel

So how do we change a person's heart? It's impossible. We might
be able to restrain a person's angry outbursts by tying him up and
gagging him, but we are powerless to change a person's heart.

This is where God's plan of redemption comes into play. The
gospel is not merely about "getting us saved," as if we simply
pray a prayer and are immediately transported into heaven. God
describes "salvation" and the transformation of the Christian life
like this:

> I will give you a new heart, and a new spirit I will
> put within you. And I will remove the heart of
> stone from your flesh and give you a heart of flesh.
> And I will put my Spirit within you, and cause you
> to walk in my statutes and be careful to obey my
> rules. (Ezek. 36:26–27)

This is a cataclysmic event. "Getting saved" is not about praying
a prayer and then continuing to live our lives as though nothing

happened. No, when God enters our lives, we are changed from the inside out.

The good news is that God has acted in the person of Jesus Christ. Through His life, death, and resurrection we are transformed, made new. Our problem lies at the core of our being, but God transforms our hearts. God literally places His Spirit within us and changes us from the inside out.

So as we come alongside the broken, hurting people God has placed in our lives, let's remember where our power comes from. These are not mere physical issues that we can correct through hard work. These are spiritual issues that run deeper than we can imagine. Yet God has supplied us with everything we need in order to fulfill His calling. The power to transform hearts and change lives comes from the Holy Spirit (John 6:63), through the Word of God (2 Tim. 3:16–17), and through prayer (James 5:16–20). As we use the Scriptures to give counsel to others, there is power (Heb. 4:12). As we pray passionately for their hearts to change, there is power. We cannot remove the lust from another's person's heart by our own efforts, but we have the Spirit of God working through us. Through the gospel, people can be set free from the enslaving power of sin (Rom. 6). Through the gospel, we are actually empowered to uproot the sin in our hearts and live in a way that pleases God (Gal. 5 and Rom. 8). Paul promised: "If *by the Spirit* you put to death the deeds of the body, you will live" (Rom. 8:13).

7. *How should the truth of the gospel and the power of the Holy Spirit affect the way we approach helping people change?*

Bearing one another's burdens is not easy, but it is also not optional. We have to face this challenge head on: a church full of isolated individuals feeling defeated by their sin and stripped of their joy was never God's plan for the church. Jesus intended for His church to advance powerfully through the centuries, full of love and joy. Jesus was clear: "I will build my church, and the gates of hell shall not prevail against it" (Matt. 16:18).

Paul reminded us that the Spirit of Him who raised Jesus Christ from the dead is working through us (Eph. 1:15–23; Rom. 8:11). God intends for His church to be a united body, not a cluster of isolated individuals. He has empowered us to bring truth and transformation into the lives of the people around us, not to be satisfied with handing out books and warm wishes. If the church is going to fulfill its God-given mission in our modern world, we are going to have to take our responsibility to one another seriously. We will have to accept His call to bear one another's burdens—even when it's messy, even when we find ourselves in over our heads.

So when a sister in Christ is speaking harmful words about another member of the church body, we will take the time to help her see the pride and lack of love in her heart and walk with her as she asks the Spirit to transform her heart on this issue. When we find a brother in Christ who is enslaved to his lustful desires, we will help him to understand the fear of the Lord and call out to God to transform his selfish desires into genuine love. Though you may not have a degree in psychology, you are still called to stand with the Christians in your life as they pursue the healing and transformation that only come through the power of the Holy Spirit.

8. *Would you say that your church body is characterized more by defeat and isolation or the power and transformation of the Holy Spirit? Why do you say that?*

9. *What steps can you take right away to help your church function more like God intended?*

Every Member Doing Its Part

The mission of your church is too important to leave to everyone else. The moment you begin to believe that your church can be healthy while you sit on the sidelines, you have given up on God's plan of redemption. God placed you in your unique situation because He wants you to minister to and with the other Christians He has placed around you. Paul's vision for the church included every Christian:

> We are to grow up in every way into him who is the head, into Christ, from whom the whole body,

joined and held together by every joint with which it is
equipped, when each part is working properly, makes
the body grow so that it builds itself up in love. (Eph.
4:15–16)

The goal of the church is to grow up in every way into the likeness
of Christ. But the church will never reach this goal unless "each part
is working properly." This doesn't mean that we will all function in
exactly the same way, but it does mean that we all have a responsibility. It also means that if you are not active in the church, you are
hurting your brothers and sisters. One paralyzed leg forces the rest
of the body to work twice as hard to make up for that leg's inactiv-
ity. God made you to be exactly who you are, and His Spirit has
empowered you with unique spiritual abilities, or "gifts." Together,
we function as one body. Until you and every person in your church
are actively ministering to the people around you, your area will not
have an accurate picture of what the church was created to be.

When we step outside of ourselves and begin bearing the burdens
of the people around us, it is time-consuming, messy, and often confusing. But it is necessary. Helping people change is what discipleship
is all about. As we help other Christians follow Jesus, we are going to
run into the temptations, lies, and idols that hold them back. It will be
difficult, but we know what Jesus has accomplished, and we know how
this story will end. We have a part to play in God's plan of redemption.
It won't always be fun, but we must be faithful to God's calling.

10. Would you say that you have been playing your part in the body
    of Christ? If so, how might you still need to grow in this? If not,

are you ready to get involved? What steps might you need to take?

11. *Spend some time in prayer. Ask God to give you confidence in the Spirit's power to use you in ministering to other people. Ask Him for the wisdom to know what to do and the discernment to recognize people who need help. Pray that God would use you and your church to continue His plan of redemption in your unique setting.*

 Watch the video for this session at multiplymovement.com.

2: The Local Church

You are on this earth to continue the mission that Jesus left for you: "Go and make disciples of all nations." But you can't do that on your own, nor are you expected to. God tells us to work together with the Christians He has placed in our lives to bring His healing and transformation into the life of the world. His plan of redemption involves the church working in unity to reach the people around.

Inside the church, this means that we devote ourselves to the members of our church body. We have a responsibility to challenge one another, to love one another, and to serve one another in a variety of ways. When every member takes this seriously, it makes for a healthy church (Eph. 4:16). And when the church functions as God intended, the results are nothing short of miraculous. The church becomes a place of healing, a picture of how God wants humanity to live.

But this vision goes beyond the people within a church body. We don't love and serve the Christians around us solely to maintain healthy churches. God's plan is bigger than that. It involves reaching out to the whole world. His plan of redemption will not be completed if we are satisfied with those who are already on the inside. An inwardly focused church is an unhealthy church. It is a dying church. Biblically, a church that fails to look at the world around it is no church at all.

Jesus was clear about His purpose on earth: "The Son of Man came to seek and to save the lost" (Luke 19:10). Similarly, our calling is focused on reaching those who don't know God:

> You are the light of the world. A city set on a hill cannot be hidden. Nor do people light a lamp and put it under a basket, but on a stand, and it gives light to all in the house. In the same way, let your light shine before others, so that they may see your good works and give glory to your Father who is in heaven. (Matt. 5:14–16)

Our focus is not inward. We live in the midst of a threatening environment, but we are more like a lighthouse than a bomb shelter. We are not called to hide from trouble but to guide others through it. We cannot fulfill our mission unless we serve one another in love, but living together in a tight-knit circle is not our ultimate goal. God has placed your church in the midst of a broader community so that He can spread His love, hope, and healing into the lives of the people around you.

1. *Would you say that your church is more inwardly focused or outwardly focused? Why do you say that?*

Known by Our Love

We know that we're supposed to love one another. The two greatest commandments are to love God and love people (Mark 12:28–31). Love is basic to what it means to be a follower of Jesus, and it should be what motivates us to reach out to the world around us. The only reason that we can love anyone else is because God loved us first (1 John 4:19). We are transformed by love because "God's love has been poured into our hearts through the Holy Spirit who has been given to us" (Rom. 5:5).

But what is the purpose of this love? Love should characterize the way we interact with one another. But why?

Because this is how the world will recognize us:

> A new commandment I give to you, that you love
> one another: just as I have loved you, you also are
> to love one another. By this all people will know
> that you are my disciples, if you have love for one
> another. (John 13:34–35)

Let's say you spent three years following Jesus closely and studying at His feet. That should make a difference in your life, right? Other people should be able to look at your life and notice a change. Something about you should signal your connection to Jesus. But the difference should not just be in our teaching or even in our pursuit of holiness. They should notice a love like they have never seen.

Jesus told His disciples that they should look different because of their love. Something about the way we love the people around us should signal to the world that we belong to Jesus. Our mission will include preaching, encouraging, rebuking, serving, studying, suffering, and many other things. But if all of these activities are not manifestations of love, then we have missed the point.

2. *Read 1 Corinthians 13. Would you say that the life of your church is characterized by love? Why or why not?*

3. *What steps can you take to be an example of love in your church? Whether you are an official leader in your church or not, how can you lead others in being more loving?*

A Compelling Community

On the night He was betrayed, Jesus prayed for His disciples. This was a pivotal moment for them, and Jesus prayed that they would be strengthened, focused, and protected. Interestingly, Jesus did not pray only for His disciples, but for "those who will believe in me through their word." In other words, *Jesus prayed for us*. Pay careful attention to what Jesus prayed on our behalf:

> I do not ask for these only, but also for those who
> will believe in me through their word, that they
> may all be one, just as you, Father, are in me, and
> I in you, that they also may be in us, so that the
> world may believe that you have sent me. The
> glory that you have given me I have given to them,
> that they may be one even as we are one, I in them
> and you in me, that they may become perfectly
> one, so that the world may know that you sent
> me and loved them even as you loved me. (John
> 17:20–23)

Jesus prayed that we would be united. Why? So that the world would believe that Jesus was sent by God, and so that the world would know that God loves us. Isn't it amazing that Jesus believed that the unity of His church would communicate all of this to the world? So often we assume that having right and logical arguments will be enough, but Jesus said the world will be convinced by our unity. And when you think about it, haven't we all heard the objections from unbelievers who point to divisions in the church as a cause for their disbelief?

Notice that Jesus's prayer assumes that our life together as Christians won't be hidden from view. Our unity is something that the world will be able to see. Nowadays, church life can become so introverted and privatized that the world never sees the way we interact with one another. If all we ever do is gather in a private building on Sundays and perhaps meet in someone's home for a midweek Bible study, the world will never know whether we are united or not. If Jesus's desire for us is to be realized, we are going to have to stop hiding from the eyes of the unbelieving world. Jesus prayed for our unity, which means that we have to focus on loving and serving each other. But we need to be doing this in such a way that the world can see what we are doing and recognize it as a picture of unity.

4. *Read John 17. Pay careful attention to Jesus's desire for His followers. Would you say that your church could be characterized by this kind of unity? Why or why not?*

5. *Take some time to think about your church and your unique cultural setting. What would it take for your church to be united, and for that unity to be displayed to the unbelieving world?*

When was the last time someone *asked you* about your faith? Most of us would have to answer "never." Why do you think that is? The New Testament assumes that people will be able to look at the church, and that they will be struck by what they see. Listen to Peter's exhortation:

> Now who is there to harm you if you are zealous for what is good? But even if you should suffer for righteousness' sake, you will be blessed. Have no fear of them, nor be troubled, but in your hearts honor Christ the Lord as holy, always being prepared to make a defense to anyone who asks you for a reason for the hope that is in you; yet do it with gentleness and respect, having a good conscience, so that, when you are slandered, those who revile your good behavior in Christ may be put to shame. (1 Pet 3:13 16)

Peter was speaking about suffering when we haven't done anything to deserve it. What should happen when we suffer for doing good? We should honor Christ in our hearts, and we should be ready to explain our hope. Peter assumed that we are going to suffer unjustly, and that when we do, we are going to respond with so much hope and joy that people will ask us what is going on. And when that happens, we should be ready to proclaim the gospel.

But it doesn't happen like that for most churches. There isn't anything compelling about the way we live together. Our love isn't very noticeable. Our unity is either nonexistent or hidden behind the doors of the fellowship hall. When we suffer, it's usually because we've done something wrong. In the rare event that we experience suffering that we didn't earn, we respond by complaining.

In other words, we don't give anyone a reason to ask about what makes us unique, so nobody asks. Yet we still feel the need to evangelize. So we end up coming across like salespeople peddling a product that didn't really work for us. We should all pray for the courage to tell others about Jesus, but we also should be working toward the love and unity that makes the church attractive. Let's not place our hope in clever sales tactics. Let's not give up on Jesus's strategy of reaching people simply because it feels impossible at times. Jesus's strategy was the life of the church. We must stick with His plan and pray that supernatural love begins to characterize our churches.

Jesus said that the world would recognize us by our love and unity. Peter said that people would be compelled by our hope. But are *love, unity,* and *hope* the words that unbelievers use when describing your church?

6. *Do you ever feel like a salesperson when sharing your faith? What steps can you take to change this?*

7. *What would it mean for your church to live as a compelling community—a group of people who demonstrate love, unity, and hope in*

such a way that the unbelieving world is compelled to find out what
is going on?

A Kingdom of Priests

As you will see in the sessions on the Old Testament, God made
a covenant with Moses and Israel. As God spoke with Moses on
Mount Sinai, He explained how Israel would relate to Him and
what it would mean for Him to live in their midst. Israel's calling and identity were clear: "You shall be my treasured possession
among all peoples, for all the earth is mine; and you shall be to
me a kingdom of priests and a holy nation" (Ex. 19:5–6). Though
all the earth belongs to God, Israel belonged to God in a special
way—they were His people. They were a holy nation, a group of
people set apart for God's purposes. And they were a kingdom of
priests. A priest represented the people to God—interceding on
their behalf—and represented God to the people—mediating His
truth, commands, and grace into their lives. Israel stood collectively as a kingdom made up of priests. They stood amid all the
nations of the earth in a priestly role, ready to represent the nations
to God and God to the nations.

When you study the New Testament, you will see that the
church is given this same vocation. "You are a chosen race, a royal
priesthood, a holy nation, a people for his own possession, that you

may proclaim the excellencies of him who called you out of darkness into his marvelous light" (1 Pet. 2:9). In God's plan of redemption, the church is called to be and to do what Israel failed to be and to do. The purpose of the church is to work together to reach out to the world around us. We have been called out of darkness into His marvelous light *so that* we can proclaim God's excellencies to a watching world.

8. *Read 1 Peter 2:4–12. How should Peter's description of our calling as the church affect the way we think about and interact with our surrounding community?*

Your Church Matters

We are called to make disciples, and strengthening the other members of the church body is an important part of this. But if we are not working together to help the unbelieving world around us become followers of Jesus, then we are missing the point of our salvation. God blessed Abraham so that He could bless the world through him (see Gen. 12). If your church is not actively blessing the surrounding community, then you are ignoring God's mission. We can never forget that we have a role to play in God's plan of redemption. You should feel honored to know that God has a plan for your church in particular.

Though God's church is meant to cover the globe, there is no church aside from the local church. God has placed you in your unique setting, alongside a unique group of Christians, for the purpose of proclaiming Him to the unbelieving world around you. The way you interact with these people matters. It doesn't matter whether your church is thousands strong or if you meet with two other Christians in a living room. It doesn't matter if your church was formed yesterday or one hundred years ago. But the way your church functions does matter. Your church is essential to God's ongoing plan of redemption. Remember that God left His church to fulfill His mission, and He didn't leave a backup plan. If your church does not pursue God's mission, then your community misses out on being exposed to the hope that God offers them in the gospel. Too many churches miss out on the vibrant life Jesus wants us to experience as we pursue His mission together.

The life of your church is a matter of life and death. God tells us how the story will end, but you have an essential role to play nonetheless. Will you help your church step up, look at the community around you with the compassion of Jesus, and call them into the plan of redemption that has transformed your church body? There's a reason God has you in this church at this point in history. You can help your church become an attractive community that exhibits Christ's love, unity, and hope.

9. *Spend some time in prayer. God's calling for your church is too important to neglect, and it's too important to take on without the power of the Spirit. Ask God to so fill the life of your church with His Spirit that your community notices a difference. Ask Him to*

equip you for the role He has called you to play in His plan of redemption.

 Watch the video for this session at multiplymovement.com.

3: The Global Church

As important as the local church is, God's plan extends way beyond your town. As much as God wants you to reach the people in your community, He has no intention of stopping there. God's plan of redemption reaches into your neighborhood—and to every other city, village, and jungle around the globe!

If your church bands together and reaches out to every individual in your community, you are still not done with God's mission. No matter how big of a revival you experience, your area is still only a small part of the world that God has sent us to transform through His gospel. Until our vision of the church encompasses the entire globe, we do not have an accurate view of God's church or His plan of redemption.

All the Families of the Earth

Let's go back to the very beginning. As soon as God's good world became corrupted by the sin of Adam and Eve, God made a promise to restore it. God told the serpent:

> I will put enmity between you and the woman,
>> and between your offspring and her offspring;
> he shall bruise your head,
>> and you shall bruise his heel. (Gen. 3:15)

The devastating influence of sin would affect all of mankind, and the struggle for redemption would be between the offspring of the woman and the offspring of the serpent. Ultimately, this promise became a reality in the person of Jesus Christ, who crushed Satan's head by dying on the cross and rising from the grave. But it is also important to see that this promise belongs to the human race. It is not confined to any ethnic group or geographical location. The promise of redemption is as broad as humanity.

God reiterated this promise to Abraham:

> I will make of you a great nation, and I will bless
> you and make your name great, so that you will be
> a blessing. I will bless those who bless you, and him
> who dishonors you I will curse, and in you all the
> families of the earth shall be blessed. (Gen. 12:2–3)

The blessing that God promised here worked itself out through Abraham's descendants: the people of Israel. Ultimately, the blessing centered upon one Israelite in particular, Jesus of Nazareth. But we have to remember that although the promise came *through* one nation, the blessing has always been intended for all nations.

God has called your church to play a role in His plan of redemption. And since His plan is a global plan, your church needs to think beyond your city limits. You can't be everywhere at once, and your resources and manpower are limited. But in order to be a part of God's mission on earth, you need to think in global terms.

1. *In your own words, why is it important to think about God's plan of redemption in global terms?*

2. *When you think about the mission of your church, does the rest of the globe factor in at all? How so?*

Where Christ Has Not Been Named

When you study the New Testament, you will look at Paul's missionary career. Though we may think of Paul as a theologian or a pastor, he was a missionary in every sense of the word. Much of the book of Acts follows Paul as he travelled—often amid great danger, difficulty, and persecution—from place to place, proclaiming the gospel and forming churches among those who responded by following Jesus.

It wasn't an accident that Paul spent so much of his life spreading the gospel to new areas. In Romans 15:20–21, Paul explained that this was his passion:

> I make it my ambition to preach the gospel, not
> where Christ has already been named, lest I build
> on someone else's foundation, but as it is written,
>
> "Those who have never been told of him will see,
>   and those who have never heard will
>   understand."

When Paul said "as it is written," he was quoting Isaiah 52, which describes Jesus as the servant of the Lord who would suffer in order to bring healing to His people. Earlier in the chapter, God clearly explained that although He was speaking directly to Israel, His salvation is for all of the nations, and He would specifically send ministers to spread this good news:

> How beautiful upon the mountains
> are the feet of him who brings good news,

who publishes peace, who brings good news of
    happiness,
who publishes salvation,
who says to Zion, "Your God reigns."
… The LORD has bared his holy arm
before the eyes of all the nations,
and all the ends of the earth shall see
the salvation of our God. (Isa. 52:7, 10)

Interestingly, Paul cited the beginning of this passage earlier in the book of Romans. Paul made clear not only that salvation is offered to all mankind but also that we are called to take an active role in spreading the gospel:

There is no distinction between Jew and Greek; for
the same Lord is Lord of all, bestowing his riches on
all who call on him. For "everyone who calls on the
name of the Lord will be saved."

How then will they call on him in whom they
have not believed? And how are they to believe in
him of whom they have never heard? And how
are they to hear without someone preaching? And
how are they to preach unless they are sent? As it is
written, "How beautiful are the feet of those who
preach the good news!" (Rom. 10:12–15)

So what does this all mean? God's plan of redemption belongs to all of humanity, yet only those who have heard the message are able to respond to it. Paul's ambition in life was to take this message of redemption and bring it to those who had never heard.

Keep in mind that Paul's passion to spread the gospel more broadly was not a personal preference. It was an essential part of the mission that Jesus gave to the church. Remember that Christ commanded us to make disciples among all nations. We misunderstand God's plan of redemption unless we see it reaching to all humanity.

3. *Take some time to think about the passages above (Romans 15:20–21, Isaiah 52:7–10, Romans 10:12–15). How should these truths affect the way we think about our calling?*

Before the End Will Come

This world will not end until God's plan is accomplished. God sends His people out into the world to embody and to proclaim His healing, and He will not wrap up human history until this has been accomplished. If His plan has always been about redeeming people from every nation on earth, then He is not content with happy, healthy churches in our communities alone—and we shouldn't be either. Though we should long to see Christ glorified in our immediate context, we should share Paul's passion to see Him glorified in every corner of the globe.

Though the details surrounding the end of the earth and the timeframe of many of the prophesies in the Bible are the subject of frequent debate, Jesus made clear that the message of the gospel should not be isolated to one part of the globe: "This gospel of the kingdom will be proclaimed throughout the whole world as a testimony to all nations, and then the end will come" (Matt. 24:14).

Many Christians are surprised to hear that there are still many groups of people around the world that have never heard the name of Jesus. We take it for granted that the people around us have access to the gospel if they ever develop an interest. Even if there's not a church or a Christian in close proximity (though this is difficult to imagine), at the very least everyone has access to gospel messages on the television, radio, or Internet. But that is simply not the case worldwide. There are people around the world who desperately need hope, healing, and salvation, but who don't have access to the message of redemption.

Paul's questions are as relevant today as they were two thousand years ago: How will they call on Him in whom they have not believed? And how are they to believe in Him of whom they have never heard? And how are they to hear without someone preaching? And how are they to preach unless they are sent?

These questions should burn in our minds and in our hearts. We are not following Jesus fully if we are not concerned about proclaiming the "gospel of the kingdom … throughout the whole world" (Matt. 24:14). This is what Jesus did while He was on earth. And now, through the power of His death and resurrection, Jesus calls us to do the same.

4. *Have you given much thought to the unreached people groups around the world? If so, how does this affect your thinking and lifestyle? If not, why do you think you have never thought about it?*

Working Together for the Gospel

Once we start developing a passion for Christ's glory to be seen around the world, we need to figure out what role we are called to play. Make no mistake, every Christian is called to be involved in spreading the gospel around the world! No one is off the hook. No one is called to a life that is separate from global missions. But this doesn't mean that we all need to immediately start packing for the jungle.

God may well want you to take His gospel overseas. Too many Christians discount that possibility too quickly. Some people are too comfortable with their current lifestyle and would never dream of sacrificing their comfort for God's glory. Others quickly assume that they are called to something else, something more normal. We shouldn't make these assumptions. Have you ever genuinely told God that you would submit yourself to His will in this area? Right now, you should ask God if He wants you to pursue living in a different location for the sake of the gospel. It may be a terrifying thought, but we have to trust God more than we trust ourselves. We are here on this earth for His glory. God has blessed you so that you will use whatever He has given you for His glory, not yours. Ultimately, we should expect God's plan to lead us places that we wouldn't naturally go.

5. *Take a minute to pause and ask God what He wants for your life. Ask Him to break through any excuses you may be hiding behind and idols you might be clinging to. Ask Him to make you willing to follow Him in whichever direction He might lead. If you have any thoughts based on this time of prayer, make a few notes below.*

We all need to consider whether God is calling us to follow Him onto the mission field, but we have to remember that this is not the only way of working to fulfill God's plan to reach every nation. If we decide that God wants us to remain in the area in which He has placed us for the time being, then we need to be using our resources to further the mission around the world. Even if we find our primary ministry in the people directly surrounding us, we need to be praying for our fellow workers in other parts of the earth. The church is spread across the world, and we need to be doing everything in our power to reach people in every corner of the globe.

John wrote a letter to a Christian man named Gaius who had been helping missionaries as they travelled to spread the gospel more broadly. His words put our role in supporting missionaries around the world in perspective:

It is a faithful thing you do in all your efforts for these brothers, strangers as they are, who testified to your love before the church. You will do well to send them on their journey in a manner worthy of God. For they have gone out for the sake of the name, accepting nothing from the Gentiles. Therefore we ought to support people like these, that we may be fellow workers for the truth. (3 John v. 5–8)

John said that "we ought to support people like these" (i.e., missionaries), and that in supporting them we are actually "fellow workers for the truth." None of us is beyond the task of missions. We are all in this together. We all have a part to play. We may never set foot in a remote jungle, but our lives should be devoted to seeing God's will be done in our neighborhoods and in Africa and Papua New Guinea. When we take up the call to follow Jesus, we are committing to making disciples in our hometowns and in the Middle East. The question is not whether or not we will be working to spread the gospel around the world, but what role we will play in this. A church that is not devoted to the cause of Christ around the world is not a church in the biblical sense.

6. *How would you describe your role in furthering the gospel around the world? If nothing comes to mind, write down a few things that you can begin to pursue in order to make missions a part of your life.*

A Vision of the End

God tells us that history is moving toward a specific and glorious end. God promised Abraham that through him all the nations of the earth would be blessed. This is what God's plan of redemption has been about from the very beginning. And when we look ahead to the end of the story, we see that God's promise to Abraham will be fulfilled. There is no doubt about whether or not the church will fulfill its mission; we know for certain that this is how the world will end.

John was actually allowed to see the fulfillment of this promise that God made to Abraham:

> After this I looked, and behold, a great multitude that no one could number, from every nation, from all tribes and peoples and languages, standing before the throne and before the Lamb, clothed in white robes, with palm branches in their hands, and crying out with a loud voice, "Salvation belongs to our God who sits on the throne, and to the Lamb!" (Rev. 7:9–10)

This is where we are headed. As distant and unfamiliar as the churches in India, Africa, China, and Papua New Guinea may seem, our future is inextricably tied to theirs. When Jesus returns to reclaim this world as its rightful King, we will find ourselves praising God alongside Christians from every age and from every nation on earth.

God's plan for our future ought to affect the way we live and think today. Does the church in China matter to you? When you hear about the persecution that Christians are enduring in other parts of the world, do you feel any compassion for them? When you hear about a mission setting off for Iraq or Thailand, do you make plans to pray for them or support them financially? These are our brothers and sisters. Their mission is the same as ours. They are working together with us toward the same goal. We cannot fulfill the mission that God has given us without them.

Jesus called His followers to be His witnesses "in Jerusalem and in all Judea and Samaria, and to the end of the earth" (Acts 1:8). We have not yet reached the end of the earth, but through the power of God's Spirit, we will. As followers of Jesus Christ, our calling is to faithfully make disciples. These disciples are also called to make disciples. Jesus promises that He will be with us as we do this, right down to the very end (Matt. 28:20). We don't know when that end will come, but we want to be faithful in making disciples until that time comes. We are God's creations, living in God's earth, placed within God's plan of redemption. May our lives be devoted to His kingdom and His glory.

7. *In order to faithfully follow Jesus and play your part in God's plan of redemption, what should your life look like right now? (This is a huge question, but try to write down a few things to guide you as you seek to put the things you've learned into practice.)*

8. *Spend some time in prayer. Ask God to help you submit to Him entirely. Ask Him to guide you and empower you in anything He calls you to do. Pray that God would use you in your neighborhood and around the world in any capacity that He sees fit.*

 Watch the video for this session at multiplymovement.com.

Part III: How to Study the Bible

1: Why Study the Bible?

As we have said, an important part of making disciples is teaching people to obey everything Jesus commanded (Matt. 28:20). This means that we need to know Jesus's teaching and commands. It may seem that the first disciples had an advantage on us here. How can we teach people to follow Jesus if we haven't observed His ministry and listened to His teaching? But we are not at a disadvantage at all because God has recorded His words and the testimony of Jesus's followers in a book—the Bible.

For a Christian, nothing should seem more natural than reading the Bible. Peter, one of Jesus's first disciples, compared it to a baby's natural craving for milk: "Like newborn infants, long for the pure spiritual milk, that by it you may grow up into salvation—if indeed you have tasted that the Lord is good" (1 Pet. 2:2–3).

As a newborn depends on milk to survive and to grow, we should equally depend on the words of Scripture for our spiritual survival and growth. The words of the Bible have impacted millions of lives over thousands of years, and God wants it to change our lives as well. If you don't already love the Bible, pray that you would.

No matter what your experience with the Bible has been, it's helpful for all of us to step back and think about what the Bible actually is. When we talk about the Bible, we sometimes use profound language without considering what we're really saying. Perhaps the strongest thing we can say about the Bible is that it is the "Word of God." But have you ever thought about what that means? That concept should blow our minds. When we talk about the Bible, we're actually talking about something that the all-powerful, all-knowing, transcendent God decided to write to us! What could be more important?

Think of how you would respond to hearing a voice from heaven speaking directly to you. We should approach the Bible with the same reverence.

If we really believe that the Bible is the Word of God, then it should be much more than a book that we are familiar with. It ought to shape every aspect of our existence. It should guide the decisions we make in life. If God is the designer and creator of this world, if He made us and placed us on this earth, and if He has taken the time to tell us who He is, who we are, and how this world operates, then what could be more important to us than the Bible?

But even after we decide that the Bible is important, we still need to learn to approach it in the right way and with the right motives. Many Christians misuse the Bible because they never ask themselves *why* they are studying it in the first place. The purpose of this session is to help you think through the nature of the Bible, why it is important to study, and how it should transform our lives.

Studying the Right Book for the Wrong Reasons

Before you go any further, ask yourself why you study the Bible. Don't be overly optimistic with this; try to assess your heart. When you pick up the Bible and begin to read it, what is motivating you? Are you driven by guilt? Do you have a desire to know God more fully? Are you looking for arguments against other perspectives? Are you looking for material for a Bible study or sermon?

1. *Take a few minutes to examine your motivations and write down a few thoughts below.*

The fact of the matter is that most Christians study the Bible for the wrong reasons. Here we will explore three motivations for studying the Bible that we need to move beyond: guilt, status, and teaching material.

Guilt

Many people are motivated by guilt. We all know that we should be reading our Bibles—it's just one of those things that Christians are told they are supposed to do. It is often added to a list with things like church attendance, tithing, and not swearing. Nobody wants to admit that they read the Bible out of guilt, but guilt is a powerful motivator.

Very often this guilt is connected with legalism. We create our own standard ("I must read x chapters per day") and then hold ourselves to it, never stopping to consider that God has not placed this standard on us, we have placed it on ourselves. It doesn't take long before we begin holding other people to that standard as well. And thus a culture of guilt is formed, a culture where "good Christians" read their Bibles because they're afraid not to, and "bad Christians" feel guilty about not meeting their Bible-reading quota.

Status

There is a certain status or air of respect reserved for those who know their Bibles well. And rightly so. We should all aspire to know God's Word inside and out. It should be on the tip of our tongues and deeply ingrained on our hearts and minds.

But take a minute to ask yourself why you want to know the Bible well. God is pleased when we treasure His Word, but do you really think He is pleased with your desire to appear intelligent? Does your desire to be the "go-to guy" who is never stumped really bring Him glory? What about your desire to be recognized as the best or the most spiritual person in the room?

It's not about studying the Bible too much (as if that were possible); it's about your motivation. Too often Christians are motivated by status when we should be motivated by a desire to know God, to be changed by His Word, and to love and serve the people around us.

Chances are, you know someone who knows the Bible inside and out. Maybe you've noticed how that person gets treated, and you want what he or she has. Competition is a great motivator, but it's the wrong reason to study the Bible. God cares more about your character than your productivity, and let's face it, studying the Bible in order to be better than someone else is ridiculous.

Teaching Material

Sometimes our motivations get skewed when we have to study the Bible in order to lead a Bible study, preach a sermon, or just have some sort of scriptural gem to share with someone. This tends to be a much more subtle misuse of the Bible. It's not wrong to use the Bible in preparation for teaching other people. In fact, it's necessary. The problem arises when we begin to approach the Bible *only* as a source for teaching material. If you are in a role where you preach or teach to others, do you find yourself simply scanning the Bible for nuggets to share? Or do you soak in the Scriptures because of what they have to say to *you*, listening to what God wants to teach *you*, allowing the Bible to transform *you* in unexpected ways?

2. *Take a minute to think about your past experience with studying the Bible. Which of the wrong motivations listed above are you guilty of? Can you think of any others?*

Why Did God Give Us the Bible?

The best place to begin in refining our motivation for studying the Bible is to ask a simple question. Why did God give us the Bible? We're used to the thought that the Bible is God's Word. But why did He give it us? If the Bible is God's Word, why did God decide to speak to us in the first place? Until we understand what the purpose of the Bible is, we are bound to keep approaching it in ways that miss God's intention.

To Teach Us about Himself

So why did God give us the Bible? One reason that seems obvious is that He wanted to describe Himself to us. From beginning to end, God is the subject of the Scriptures. Everything in this book is God centered. Genesis begins with a God who existed alone and then spoke all things into existence. Revelation ends with this same God reigning eternally over all that He created. Every book in between reveals His character and attributes by narrating His sovereign actions throughout history.

God in heaven wants us to know certain things about Himself, and He uses the Scriptures to reveal these things. People naturally want to believe in a human-centered world, so God gave us the Bible, which shows that everything revolves around God. He is the First and the Last, the King of kings, and Lord of lords. He is described as "holy," which speaks to the massive disparity between God and people. It is important to God that we understand this.

It is through the Bible that we learn about God's power, justice, mercy, wrath, love, kindness, anger, faithfulness, jealousy, holiness, compassion, etc. Because God is already described in the Bible, we are left with no room to formulate our own opinions. We should all study in order to understand God better. We search diligently to know the truth about God and to rid ourselves of any misconceptions we hold about Him.

To Teach Us about Ourselves and the World We Live In

God also gave us the Bible so that we can understand the world we live in. It is a grand narrative that explains where we came from, why the world is the way it is, and where everything is headed. It explains who we are as human beings and how we should think about our existence.

Many Christians think that the Bible is helpful for answering religious questions and teaching us how to live godly lives, but it doesn't have answers for the tough questions that we face in philosophy, science, or sociology. This is not true! The Bible gives us answers to all of life's most important questions. The Bible gives us much more than "religious truths"; it accurately explains the world we live in. The God who wrote the Bible is the God who designed this world. Since this is His world, it only makes sense to view the world from His perspective and live according to His principles.

All of this means that as we study the Bible, we should be seeking to understand our God, our world, and ourselves. Rather than pursuing an emotional experience or trying to accumulate religious knowledge, we should be learning to live in the world that God made.

To Enable Us to Live Godly Lives

Another reason that God gave us the Bible is to enable us to live godly lives. Peter said that God's "divine power has granted to us all things that pertain to life and godliness, through the knowledge of him who called us to his own glory and excellence" (2 Pet. 1:3). Simply put, through the knowledge of God we gain everything we need for living godly lives. Whatever motivations we may have for studying the Bible, godly living needs to be near the top of that list. We study because we want to be godly.

Paul said that "All Scripture is breathed out by God and profitable for teaching, for reproof, for correction, and for training in righteousness, *that the man of God may be complete, equipped for every good work*" (2 Tim. 3:16–17). First, Paul said that Scripture is literally "breathed out" by God. Though He used human authors to write each book of the Bible, God Himself is the ultimate source of these words. But notice the purpose statement that Paul included: "that the man of God may be complete, equipped for every good work." So why did God give us the Bible? He gave it to us *so that* we would be complete, mature people who are equipped and ready to do anything God asks us to do.

This means that as we study the Bible, we should be looking to change. Hebrews 4:12 warns us that "the word of God is living and active, sharper than any two-edged sword, piercing to the division of soul and of spirit, of joints and of marrow, and discerning the thoughts and intentions of the heart." Though we primarily think of the Bible as something we read in order to gain knowledge, we actually have it backward. The Bible reads us—it penetrates to our core and exposes who we really are. If you ever find yourself reading your Bible and not changing, then you can be sure that you're approaching the Bible in the wrong way. It's not about finding support for our lifestyle or way of thinking; it's about approaching the mind of God and letting Him change and redefine who we are.

To Facilitate a Relationship with God

God wants you to know Him, and He gave you the Scriptures so that you can. Every relationship requires communication—the loving expression of each person's thoughts, emotions, concerns, and dreams that strengthens the relationship and deepens intimacy. This is how our relationships with one another function, so why would it be any different with God? The Bible is His means of sharing His thoughts and desires with us! We are relational beings because He created us that way. He Himself exhibits pure relationship in the perfect union and love between the members of the Trinity. From the day He placed Adam in the garden, God has maintained a relationship with mankind, and communication has always been central to that relationship.

When we open the Bible, therefore, we are engaging with God's communication to us. He chose specific words to say to specific people at specific times. He chose sixty-six books to preserve for us so that we could know Him better. Though different parts of the Bible are addressed to different people, everything in the Bible is ultimately written for our benefit. If the Bible is indeed "breathed out by God"—words delivered from the mouth of God Himself—then reading the Bible is listening to the voice of God.

Every time we read the Bible we are strengthening our relationship with God—unless we approach the Bible for the wrong reasons. If we approach the Bible with humility, eagerly listening for God to speak to us, waiting to hear what God has to say rather than what we want to hear, then we are drawing closer to the one we were made to be in relationship with. True Bible study must always have intimacy with God as a primary goal.

To Exalt Jesus

God uses the Scriptures to explain how and why He has exalted Jesus to the highest place. All of the events in biblical history point to His Son. The law was given to show us our sinfulness and our need for Jesus. Old Testament priests and sacrifices point to our need for the greater high priest and ultimate sacrifice. The Gospels record the loving words and actions of the Son of God. The epistles explain how it is only through His work on the cross that we can be saved from sin and filled with the Spirit. Revelation shows how He will one day return to judge and restore the earth, and reign with His followers forever. All of this is written to exalt Jesus to the glory of God the Father. These words should move us to exalt Jesus in our everyday lives.

To Prepare Us for Our God-Given Mission

From the very beginning, God has had a mission for humanity. After God finished creating the world and everything in it, He created the first man and placed him in the garden "to work it and keep it" (Gen. 2:15). God also gave humanity dominion over the creation. Whatever it means for people to have "dominion" over the creation, it does not mean that we have the right to destroy the creation in any way that serves our purpose. Instead, if humanity's dominion is to look anything like God's dominion, then our responsibility is to lovingly care for the world that God made. From the moment Adam was created by God, people have had a mission on this earth.

God chose Abraham to be the father of the nation of Israel. God blessed Abraham, promised to make him into a great nation, and said, "in you all the families of the earth shall be blessed" (Gen. 12:3). When we think about the nation of Israel, we often think that God chose them so that they could be separated from the rest of the world, enjoying God's blessings and living their lives as God's "favorites." But from the moment He chose Abraham, God made it clear that Abraham was to look outward with the blessings he had been given. Abraham was blessed *so that* he could be a blessing to all of the nations of the earth. Israel's mission was to show the world who their God was.

In the New Testament, the mission of God's people becomes even clearer. We are not on this earth merely to enjoy our own personal relationships with God. We are here to be God's servants, His ambassadors: "Therefore, we are ambassadors for Christ, God making his appeal through us. We implore you on behalf of Christ, be reconciled to God" (2 Cor. 5:20).

Though much of Christian thought tells us that we are the center of it all—that it's all about you and God and nothing else really matters—the reality is that God is the center, and He has saved us so that we can work with Him in His mission to redeem humanity and restore creation to what He originally intended it to be.

This means that when we read the Bible, we need to view it as our marching orders. Rather than coming to the Bible with our own agenda and trying to find verses that support what we'd like to do, we need to allow the Bible to shape our hopes and dreams. Every time we read the Bible, we should understand our mission a little better. Why are we on this earth in the first place? How can we take part in what God is doing in this world? These are all questions that the Bible answers—as long as we are ready to listen.

3. *Take a minute to think through why God gave us the Bible. How should these things affect the way you think about studying the Bible?*

Approaching the Mind of God

Ultimately, when we read the Bible, we are approaching the mind of God. Every time you open the Bible, you ought to prepare yourself for an encounter with the Creator of the universe. So how do you prepare yourself for this type of encounter?

It should go without saying that we ought to approach God with humility. We know that we ought to be humble with other people and with God, but we don't usually think of being humble with the

Bible. We make this mistake because we don't think about what it is that we're doing when we read our Bibles. Reading your Bible with humility means that you're assuming the role of a student. Too often we search the Bible to find agreement with the views we already hold. This is backward. Instead, we need to recognize that we know nothing.

We don't have the answers—that's why we're reading the Bible.

Approaching the Bible with humility means that we're laying aside our agendas and looking for what God will teach us. Every time you find yourself struggling to accept something the Bible says, you've found an area of your life that needs to be brought into submission to Christ. Unfortunately, we often waste these opportunities by finding ways to explain away what the Bible is saying to us.

And that's the real test—when you find that your beliefs or lifestyle don't match the Bible, do you assume that the Bible is wrong? Every time we find ourselves disagreeing with God, we can be certain that we are the ones who need to change. God didn't give us the Bible to help us feel better about the way we do things; He wrote the Bible to tell us what He wants us to be and do. Until we begin reading the Bible in order to draw close to God and do what He says, we are completely missing the point.

4. *How do you tend to respond to the Bible's teaching? Would you say that you approach it humbly with a desire to change? How do you need to adjust your approach to studying the Bible?*

Right Motivation Makes All the Difference

In 1 Corinthians 8, Paul talked about food offered to idols. The pagan religions at that time would offer meat to their idols. After the ceremony, they would take the meat (obviously the idols didn't eat it) and sell it in the marketplace at a reduced price. Understandably, some Christians who had converted from paganism had a problem with eating this meat because they felt as if they were participating in idolatry by doing so. Other Christians rightly understood that these idols were nothing, and they could eat that meat with a clear conscience.

The problem came, however, when these Christians began to use their knowledge to push their brothers and sisters to act against their consciences. In addressing that issue, Paul said these profound words: "Now concerning food offered to idols: we know that 'all of us possess knowledge.' This 'knowledge' puffs up, but love builds up" (1 Cor. 8:1).

Paul's warning serves as a great case in point for what happens when we study the Bible with the wrong motives. When we study the Bible in order to gain more knowledge, to look more intelligent, to prove a point to someone else, or to convince other people that they should think and act just as we do, then we are studying the Bible with wrong motives. And what is the fruit of this type of study? We become "puffed up." Ironically—tragically—the act of studying the Bible has produced some of the most arrogant people this world has ever seen. Chances are, you know one or two of these people.

5. *Rather than thinking about all of the arrogant people you know, take a minute to consider whether or not your efforts in studying*

the Bible have simply puffed you up. How has studying the Bible
changed you? Are you more arrogant, argumentative, or judgmental?
Write down a few thoughts below:

Clearly, this is not the way God wants us to study the Bible. Instead,
reading God's Word should lead us to become more like God. As
Paul said, knowledge puffs up, but love builds up. When we come
to the Bible without an agenda, looking for the ways in which God
wants to teach us and change us, then we will walk away more like
the people that God desires us to be.

Remember Peter's exhortation: "So put away all malice and all
deceit and hypocrisy and envy and all slander. Like newborn infants,
long for the pure spiritual milk, that by it you may grow up into salvation" (1 Pet. 2:1–2). We should set aside every ungodly desire and
inclination and simply long to be fed and nourished by the Word
of God. It's a very simple concept that brings life-changing results.
Imagine how different you would be if you aligned your thinking
and lifestyle with the Bible. Rather than becoming arrogant, you
would love God more; you would be in tune with your God-given
mission; you would see people not as means to your own ends but as
valuable creations of God, and you would find ways to love and serve
the people around you.

6. *Take a minute to meditate on 1 Peter 2:1–2. What would your life look like if you desired the Word as Peter described?*

Before You Move On

To sum it all up, the right way to approach the Bible is to first let go of everything that we want and expect, and to let God tell us exactly what to think and what to do. Of course, this is contrary to our natural tendencies, so we need God to work in our hearts to remove our poor motivations and give us a pure longing for His Word. In the next sessions, we will talk about methods for studying the Bible carefully. But before you develop skills in studying the Bible, it's absolutely essential that you work through your motivation for studying in the first place. Unless your heart is right, you will misuse the Bible, no matter how skilled you are at studying it carefully.

7. *Close this session by praying. Ask God to purify your heart with regard to Scripture. Ask Him to produce in you a longing for the pure milk of the Word.*

Watch the video for this session at multiplymovement.com.

2: Studying the Bible Prayerfully and Obediently

Is there a "right" way to study the Bible?

We will probably all agree that studying the Bible is critical, but we may not agree on the best method of study. There is no universally accepted pattern for how Christians should interact with this book. Some approach the Bible as a textbook or rulebook that gives them direction for how to live their lives. Others gravitate toward the stories and characters in the Bible as an inspiration or model for living a godly life. Still others take a more mystical approach: let it fall open to any page and you will find some spiritual encouragement or guidance to help you through the day. And then there's the academic approach, which carefully examines each passage of Scripture to determine precisely what the original authors intended to say.

Most of us cycle through each of these approaches and several others in our attempt to get the most out of the Bible. We know that we need the Bible, but we sometimes struggle in our quest to get the most out of our reading.

1. *Describe your experience with studying the Bible. What approaches have you tried? What has been effective? What has been ineffective? What have you learned in the process?*

Studying the Bible Devotionally

Before we decide on the best approach to studying the Bible, let's not forget what the Bible is: God's Word. It is His words to us, so we should be mindful of His authority as He conveys His purpose and will to us. When we read the Bible we are hearing the voice of God.

So how should we read a book that carries the same weight as the audible voice of God coming down from heaven? Obviously, we should read the Bible carefully, paying close attention to what exactly God is saying—a concept we will explore in the next session. In this session, we will focus on another important point: we should read these words devotionally. In other words, we should be "devoted" to them. When God speaks to us, we should be quick to listen, eager to absorb everything He tells us. And we should enjoy the process.

Have you ever thought to simply *enjoy reading the Bible*? We often get so caught up in the busyness of our lives or the details of the biblical text that we forget that we should be thrilled. We are hearing God's words to us!

If you want to get a feel for what it means to enjoy the Bible, then read Psalm 119. It's basically a love letter written to God's Word. Two things are particularly striking about this psalm: (1) The psalmist had a lot to say about God's Word (it's 176 verses long!), and (2) he really, really liked it. The repeated refrain is that he *delights* in God's law, statues, precepts, commandments, etc. At one point (vs. 131) he even said, "I open my mouth and pant, because I long for your commandments." That's a serious desire!

Recall once again Peter's exhortation to long for the Word of God as a baby longs for its mother's milk (1 Pet. 2:2–3). If these statements reflect the attitude a Christian should have toward the Bible, then it's safe to say that all of us are falling very short.

We should approach the Bible with the same intensity, aware of the fact that we are reading God's words, and that His words are directed to us. God has given us the Bible to use in discipling, counseling, teaching, and encouraging the people around us (see 2 Tim. 3:16–17). But whatever else we do with the Bible, we cannot fail to read the Bible devotionally. As we study the Bible to teach, correct, or encourage other people, we need to let God's truths saturate every aspect of our minds, hearts, and lifestyles.

2. *What does it look like to take joy in reading the Bible? Have you ever experienced this? If so, what is it like? If not, why do you think you've never enjoyed the Bible?*

3. *Read through Psalm 119. What do you find striking, challenging, or encouraging?*

Prayer and Understanding

Christians often talk about praying *and* reading their Bibles, but we don't hear much about praying *while* reading the Bible. While many Christians will acknowledge that prayer is an important part of understanding Scripture, not many of us have done a good job of actually putting this into practice.

Some believe that if we examine the biblical text closely enough—possibly even learning Hebrew and Greek—if we consult enough commentaries, and if we diagram every passage perfectly, then we can arrive at the true meaning of any biblical text. Each of these elements is important, but this mentality leaves no room for prayer, which means that there is no dependence on the Holy Spirit. It is a mentality of complete self-reliance.

Paul's description of the difference between human wisdom and the wisdom of God is worth quoting at length:

> As it is written,

> "What no eye has seen, nor ear heard,
>   nor the heart of man imagined,

> what God has prepared for those who love
>   him"—

> these things God has revealed to us through the
> Spirit. For the Spirit searches everything, even the
> depths of God. For who knows a person's thoughts
> except the spirit of that person, which is in him?
> So also no one comprehends the thoughts of God
> except the Spirit of God. Now we have received not
> the spirit of the world, but the Spirit who is from
> God, that we might understand the things freely
> given us by God. And we impart this in words
> not taught by human wisdom but taught by the
> Spirit, interpreting spiritual truths to those who are
> spiritual.
>
> The natural person does not accept the things
> of the Spirit of God, for they are folly to him, and
> he is not able to understand them because they are
> spiritually discerned. (1 Cor. 2:9–14)

Make sure you understand the point of that passage: you *cannot* understand the Bible without the Holy Spirit's help.

Dependence on God in our thinking is a fundamental aspect of being human—and was even before the fall. When Adam and Eve were in the garden of Eden, they needed God to tell them what to do. This is huge! Even before sin entered the world, people needed revelation from God in order to understand the world they were living in. Part of what it means to be human is that we depend on revelation from God in order to understand our existence. And this dependency only intensified after the fall.

As a result of the fall, people are corrupt not only in their actions, but also in their minds (Rom. 1:21). That means we naturally stray from God morally (a concept we're all pretty familiar with), but in addition to that, our minds are tainted by sin. We no longer think the way we ought to think. This intensifies our dependence on the Spirit of God to help us see God's truth as it really is, not as we'd like it to be.

And this is exactly Paul's point: we simply cannot understand spiritual truths apart from the Spirit of God. Without the Spirit, we will look at God's revelation in nature and in the Bible and misinterpret it.

This is why prayer is absolutely essential to Bible study. It's not a symbolic gesture; it's not a formality: it is foundational to understanding the mind of God. If the Bible is God's Word, then understanding the Bible means understanding the mind of God (not fully, of course, but insofar as He has revealed His mind to us). And Paul said explicitly that the only way we can understand the mind of God is through the Spirit of God.

If our Bible study is not saturated in prayer, then we are not studying the Bible the way God intends. The Scriptures are full of the wisdom of God, and we are absolutely dependent on the Spirit to reveal that wisdom to us and establish it in our lives.

4. *In practical terms, what does it mean to study the Bible prayer-fully? What can you do to build prayer and dependence on God into your study of the Bible?*

Studying the Bible Obediently

Perhaps the strongest reason for saturating our Bible study in prayer is that we desperately need the Spirit to make our lives align with the truths we are studying. We don't need statistics to convince us that churchgoers tend toward hypocrisy. We all know people who are passionate about the truth but don't seem to understand the concept of practicing what they preach. What we need is the Spirit to keep us from becoming one of them.

What is the value of truth if it doesn't change us? Paul said it this way:

> If I speak in the tongues of men and of angels, but have not love, I am a noisy gong or a clanging cymbal. And if I have prophetic powers, and understand all mysteries and all knowledge, and if I have all faith, so as to remove mountains, but have not love, I am nothing. (1 Cor. 13:1–2)

If you could amaze people with your ability to speak, if you understood everything and had more faith than anyone on earth, but you didn't love your neighbor as yourself, then what would be the point? This is why prayer is critical. We need Him to make us loving—to make our knowledge translate into loving action.

Too many Christians study the Word of God as if gaining knowledge is the sum total of our mission on this earth. But according to Paul, knowledge can be completely worthless and even harmful: knowledge puffs up, but love builds up (1 Cor. 8:1).

If we believe that statement, then why do we have so much admiration for people who know lots of facts? Have we forgotten that knowledge is a means to a greater end? Knowledge enables us to love God and love our neighbors more fully.

If we're not putting what we know to work in our lives, then our knowledge will simply make us more arrogant. There's a terrifying irony here: *your study of the Bible could actually lead you further away from the Lord.*

The problem definitely isn't solved by studying less. Instead, we should be learning everything we can and immediately applying it. We should be begging God to give us a deeper love for Him and others so we can take the truths He reveals and put them into practice. Very often, the truths we learn will actually lead us to search for situations in which to apply them (such as caring for the poor or considering other people better than ourselves).

We can't afford to overlook this point. If you find yourself studying the Bible without applying what you're learning, then you're misusing the Bible. It's that simple—and that serious.

You may not consider yourself a biblical scholar, but think about all the things you do know about the Bible. The Bible is filled with God's commands, and you probably already know some of the things that He clearly wants you to do. Start there. Pray, obey, and begin enjoying the peace that comes from studying the Bible obediently.

5. *Take a minute to think through the commands that you know God wants us all to be doing (for example, loving the people around you, forgiving others, praying, etc.). Write down a handful of these things below.*

Now evaluate your life in light of these commands. If you find that the things you listed above aren't an active part of your life, then it's pretty evident that you need to change the way you study the Bible. If these things are not manifested in the way you live, then you're misusing the Bible. Putting our knowledge into practice will be a lifelong pursuit for all of us, and we rarely see dramatic, immediate results. But if you're not seeing the things you learn translating into the things you do, then something foundational is out of place.

6. *Take a minute to examine your life in light of what you already know about the Bible. If you find that you haven't been applying biblical truth to your life, then what changes do you need to make to the way you study the Bible?*

Studying the Bible with Faith

Something that is often overlooked when studying the Bible is the importance of faith. Once again, this goes back to the very nature of the Bible. If the Bible is indeed the very words of God, then those words carry the same authority and power as God Himself. Every promise is backed by a person—the promise is as trustworthy as the person who makes that promise. When the Bible gives us a command, that command carries all the authority of God. Likewise, when the Bible makes a promise, that promise is as trustworthy as God.

One of the church's greatest handicaps is that Christians don't study the Bible with faith. We read the Bible, but we don't act as if we believe what it says. We read about judgment for those who deny Jesus, but it doesn't change the way we reach out to the people around us. This raises the question: Do we really believe (i.e., have faith) in what God has said? Another example is when we read of God's grace. The Bible is clear that God forgives (Eph. 2:1–9, 1 John 1:9), yet many of us walk around with doubts and insecurities based upon past actions. If we studied with faith, wouldn't we live with visible peace and joy?

If we are going to study the Bible as the very words of God, then we need to believe what it says. We need to study the Bible with absolute faith. When we read that God works all things according to the counsel of His will (Eph. 1:11), then we need to believe it and live as though it were true. When we read that the Holy Spirit empowers us to put to death the deeds of the body (Rom. 8:13), then we need to put our complete confidence in that truth and live as people who are empowered by the very Spirit of God.

7. *In your own words, explain what it means to study the Bible with faith. Do you see this playing out in your life? How so?*

The Bible and Transformation

Often people come out of study groups saying, "That was a good Bible study." But what do they actually mean by that? Does it mean that they learned something or felt convicted at points? Or do they say this because their lives actually changed? Good Bible study leads to transformation. It may not happen all at once, but we should be noticeably different because of our time with Scripture.

We've already looked briefly at Hebrews 4:12: "The word of God is living and active, sharper than any two-edged sword, piercing to the division of soul and of spirit, of joints and of marrow, and discerning the thoughts and intentions of the heart." The Bible isn't merely an inanimate object that we study and pull information from. It has a life of its own. It acts. *It reads us*; it pierces to the deepest parts of our being and discerns our motivations. Since our God is a living God, His Word is alive, and He works through His Word to actively transform every part of our being.

James used striking imagery to highlight our need to be transformed by the Bible:

> But be doers of the word, and not hearers only, deceiving yourselves. For if anyone is a hearer of the word and not a doer, he is like a man who looks intently at his natural face in a mirror. For he looks at himself and goes away and at once forgets what he was like. But the one who looks into the perfect law, the law of liberty, and perseveres, being no hearer who forgets but a doer who acts, he will be blessed in his doing. (1:22–25)

James compared the process of studying the Bible to a man looking into a mirror. Just like a mirror, the Bible has the ability to reveal to you the truth about your condition. First, he described a man who looks into the mirror, clearly sees the reflection, and then walks away without doing anything. This person is clearly foolish, but he also perfectly represents the way most Christians study the Bible. They read their Bibles, see the truth that demands transformation, then walk away as if nothing ever happened.

James contrasted this fool with the person who looks into the mirror and does something about what he sees. This person reads the Word of God, takes what he sees at face value, and then acts on it. James is clear that this person is the one who will be blessed in what he does. There is no reward for merely hearing the truth. Bible study is incomplete and illegitimate until it turns into obedience and transforms us.

So again we have to ask the question: Why do you study the Bible? Is it because you want to be changed, or are you studying to gain knowledge?

James followed his powerful metaphor with these startling words:

> If anyone thinks he is religious and does not bridle his tongue but deceives his heart, this person's religion is worthless. Religion that is pure and undefiled before God, the Father, is this: to visit orphans and widows in their affliction, and to keep oneself unstained from the world. (James 1:26–27)

Once again, he pointed out that there are going to be those who "deceive themselves." Don't be one of them. If you think you are a religious person, but don't act on God's truth, Scripture says your "religion" is worthless. Don't kid yourself—true religion is not about what you know, it's about putting what you know about God and His Word into practice.

God has been so gracious to speak to us. His words lead to life. They set us free! So much of God's blessing comes to us as we listen to His voice and put His Word into practice. It would be a shame if we merely studied and didn't allow these words to bless us as He intended.

8. *Take a minute to consider everything you've thought through in this session. What changes do you need to make in the way you study the Bible?*

9. *Spend some time in prayer. Ask God to give you a heart for His Word. Ask Him to help you approach His Word devotionally and obediently.*

Watch the video for this session at multiplymovement.com.

3: Studying Logically

As we said in the previous session, an academic study of Scripture does not ensure a proper interpretation. If studying the Bible were all about academics, then our best bet would be to find the most intelligent person we know, and have him or her interpret it for us.

But while it's true that rigorous study does not guarantee right results, it does not mean that hard work and a logical approach to Scripture is insignificant. Not only is it helpful, it is necessary and commanded:

> Do your best to present yourself to God as one
> approved, a worker who has no need to be ashamed,
> rightly handling the word of truth. (2 Tim. 2:15)

God calls you to "do your best." Laziness is inexcusable. We are studying the very words that God chose to communicate to us, so in addition to studying prayerfully and obediently, we must study diligently. God calls us to love Him with our minds (Matt. 22:37), so it is an act of worship to use our minds to understand His thoughts, which in turn will lead us to love Him even more.

We tend to listen carefully when there are consequences for not listening. It's like misunderstanding driving directions and ending up lost and frustrated. How much more important is it to truly understand what God is telling you? As Christians, we claim to base our lives upon the teaching of the Bible. But what if we misunderstand that teaching?

The fact of the matter is that we all misunderstand certain passages of Scripture. If we all understood the Bible perfectly, we would all agree on every point of doctrine. Clearly this is not the case. There are many factors that lead us to misunderstand what the Bible is saying: our own assumptions, blindly following the views of people who have been influential in our lives, our sinful desire to do our own thing, etc. All of these factors are only intensified when we don't pay close attention to what the Bible is actually saying, rather than what we think it must be saying.

It is good for us to keep in mind some general principles for interpreting Scripture.

Consider the Context

Every text belongs to a context. Every chapter, paragraph, sentence, and word derives meaning from its relationship to the words, sentences, paragraphs, and chapters around it. This is true in reading ordinary books, and it is certainly true in reading the Bible.

Consider the simple word *ship*. We all know what the word means (and even if we didn't, we could easily find its definition in a dictionary). But *ship* means different things in different contexts. How do you decide whether *ship* is referring to a large boat or to the process of sending something? You look at the context. This isn't a complicated process, but it is absolutely essential in determining the meaning of the word.

We don't usually think about this because reading words in their context is second nature to us—it probably hasn't even occurred to you that you're thinking in terms of context right now, as you read these sentences. As you read, you are deciding what these words mean based on the words around them. When you run into an ambiguous word (like the word "read" in the last two sentences, which could be taken as past or present tense, depending on the context), you automatically choose the appropriate definition or tense based on the context.

The point of using these simple examples is to highlight an essential aspect of studying the Bible: in order to understand a particular word, verse, chapter, or book, we need to consider it in light of its context. Too often, verses are read and quoted in isolation. While this is not necessarily wrong, it greatly increases the chances of misinterpretation.

Here's a helpful way to get the point across: when studying Scripture, think apple rather than orange. Typically, when you eat an apple, you take a bite out of the whole fruit. When you eat an orange, you break it into isolated pieces and then eat the pieces individually. Whenever we read a verse, we should be mindful that we are taking a thought (a "bite") from a larger story. Always keep in mind that every verse is connected to a chapter, a book, and the entire Bible.

One of the best things we can do to understand context is to read the Bible in its entirety. Some choose to do this every two years, others on a yearly basis, and others even more frequently. Whatever approach you take to reading the Bible, the more often you read it, the better you will understand the whole story.[1]

1.   *Think about the way you tend to study the Bible. Would you say that you make an effort to seek out what the Bible is actually saying? Do you pay attention to the context? If so, how has this helped you? If not, how do you think this might change the way you read the Bible?*

---

1   Refer to multiplymovement.com for reading guides that will help you get into a habit of reading through the Bible regularly. If you are interested in resources that will help you place individual portions of the Bible in their context, consider using a study Bible, such as *The ESV Study Bible* (Wheaton: Crossway, 2008). Another excellent resource that will help you understand the overall story of the Bible is Craig G. Bartholomew and Michael W. Goheen, *The Drama of Scripture: Finding Our Place in the Biblical Story* (Grand Rapids: Baker Academic, 2004).

Know the Difference between Interpretation and Application

Maybe the most common mistake made in Bible interpretation is when people focus too much on "what this verse means *to me*." It's not uncommon for Bible study groups to go around the circle as each person shares an individualized interpretation. Often these interpretations are made with little study and are heavily influenced by opinion and desire. Many times, the various interpretations are incompatible with one another. In this type of setting, the focus is not on what God is saying through the Bible. Instead, each person is focused on what he or she thinks the verse means. Whether it's clearly articulated or not, this approach reveals the assumption that the Bible has a personalized meaning for each Christian. It might mean one thing to me, but another thing to you.

I don't want to completely disparage this approach. For one thing, many biblical passages have nuances of meaning, and you might notice something that others miss. In that sense, "going around the circle" can be a very helpful exercise. But this is not the same thing as saying that the Bible has a personalized meaning for each of us. Once we head down that road, there is no longer such a thing as "misinterpretation," and people are free to make the Scripture say anything. It's important to understand that the Bible means what God intends for it to mean. When we ask our children to wash the dishes, we have a clear message we want to get across, and we expect them to figure out what we mean by that statement. In the same way, God has a message to get across, and we all need to work together in order to examine God's words and find out what He is really saying to us.

Sometimes when we talk about "what this passage means to me," we are actually talking about application, rather than interpretation. With *interpretation*, we are asking what the passage is saying and what it means. With *application*, we are applying that meaning to our specific situation. Ultimately, each passage has one meaning, but it might have many different applications.

For example, in Matthew 22:39, Jesus quoted Leviticus 19:18, which says, "You shall love your neighbor as yourself." The meaning is pretty easy to grasp: we need to love the people whom God has placed around us. But how do we apply that truth to our lives? One person might apply it by helping a neighbor with her yard work, and another person might apply it by listening graciously to a coworker as he shares his concerns about his family. They might each apply the same truth to their lives in different ways tomorrow.

Application depends on our specific life situations, so we may all read the same passage and walk away with different applications. *Interpretation*, on the other hand, is all about discovering what God has actually said and what He intended to communicate. We should all read the same passage and walk away with the same meaning.

2. *In your own words, why is it important to distinguish between interpretation and application?*

Find the Plain Meaning

Sometimes our personal agendas or assumptions divert us from what God is saying in a biblical passage. For example, in Luke 12:33, Jesus said, "Sell your possessions, and give to the needy." We will often read a verse like that and say, "Okay, obviously God is not asking me to *literally* sell my possessions and give to the needy. This passage must mean _____." Really? Because it sure seems that Jesus is saying that these disciples should literally sell their possessions and give to the needy. In fact, looking at the context of Jesus's teaching and ministry only strengthens the literal meaning of that passage. Based on the rest of the book of Luke, this is exactly the sort of thing that Jesus would call His followers to do.

The fact that Jesus called His disciples to sell some possessions at that moment in history does not necessarily mean that every Christian has to sell every possession at all times, but the point is that our own agendas can keep us from even considering such a thing. If Jesus called His disciples to sell some of their stuff and use that money to meet the needs of the poor, shouldn't we be open to His calling us to do the same thing today?

We need to learn to take Scripture at face value. While some sections of the Bible are difficult to understand (2 Pet. 3:16), so much of the Bible is easily understood. When we read that "those who are in the flesh cannot please God" (Rom. 8:8), we will have to carefully study the verse and its context to decide what it means to be "in the flesh," but the plain meaning of the verse is clear: God does not want us to be in the flesh.

Other passages are more difficult. What happens when we read one of the many portions of the Old Testament that seem so distant?

In Exodus 17, for example, Israel goes to war against Amalek. As Joshua lead the army in battle, Moses sat on top of a hill and kept his hands raised in the air. The Bible says, "Whenever Moses held up his hand, Israel prevailed, and whenever he lowered his hand, Amalek prevailed" (Ex. 17:11). This is a fascinating account, but how do we interpret it? We will probably all agree that the verse isn't telling us to go sit on a hilltop and hold our hands in the air. Should we be seeking a spiritual meaning that lies beneath the surface, then? Maybe the verse means that we must keep our hands and our hearts pointed toward heaven if we are going to defeat our spiritual enemies. While that may be true, there is no indication that this is what God is telling us through this passage.

If we are going to take this verse at face value, we will read it as a description of the unusual way in which God used Moses to lead Israel to victory in a historical battle over the Amalekites. Through that story we can gain insight into the power of God and His ability to save His people, but those insights do not change the clear meaning of what God recorded in Exodus 17. It might seem more "spiritual" to try to find some deeper meaning behind the text, but what could be more spiritual than simply taking God at His word?

The Bible is a fascinating book. It is the communication of the Creator of the universe to His people. God wrote the Bible using human language, in words that we understand and use every day. He chose to communicate through a book, and He obviously has the ability to communicate His message clearly.

If we say that we shouldn't take God's words at face value, that we need to discover some sort of hidden meaning beneath the plain meaning of the words of Scripture, then we are saying that God is using human language in a way that is different from the way human beings use language. But we have absolutely no indication that this is the case. To the contrary, when God spoke to human beings in the Bible, they understood Him and acted according to the plain meaning of His words. When God told Israel to build a tabernacle, they didn't perform some sort of dance as a spiritual interpretation of His words. Instead, they took His words at face value and created a tabernacle in accordance with the plain meaning of God's words. Our approach to Scripture should be the same.

3. *In your own words, why is it important to look for the plain mean-ing of each passage rather than seeking out a deeper meaning?*

4. *Would you say that your study of the Bible is focused on finding the plain meaning of each passage? Why or why not?*

Take the Bible Literally

There is an old statement that is worth repeating here: if the literal sense makes sense, seek no other sense. We need to be careful with this, because we are still left to determine when the literal sense actually makes sense. But it makes an important point: we should look for the plain meaning of the words of Scripture. When we examine each word, verse, chapter, and book, we need to allow the context to suggest whether that verse should be taken as a literal statement, a rhetorical question, a figure of speech, etc.

Accepting the Bible as literal truth does not mean that we interpret every passage literally. When we read the Bible, we find many places where the author uses metaphors, parables, poems, prophecies, and other literary devices. For example, when Jesus said, "I am the door" (John 10:9), He was using a metaphor. We understand that He was not claiming to be made of wood and attached to a doorframe. Jesus was conveying literal truth, but using a figure of speech to do so.

But notice that this is not using any sort of strange spiritual or allegorical interpretation. We are following the normal usage of human language, which allows for metaphor, imagery, and other rhetorical devices. So when we say that we need to take the Bible literally, we need to be careful to understand what we're really saying. What we mean is that we will take the Scriptures at face value, and when the context suggests that the author is using a figure of speech or some sort of poetic or prophetic imagery, then we will follow the normal rules of human language and interpret the passage accordingly.

Don't misunderstand—this isn't always a simple task. As an illustration, consider the fact that whole camps have formed over which portions of the book of Revelation should be read literally and which should be read figuratively. We will often disagree over which specific passages are speaking literally and which ones are using rhetorical devices. This means that we need to be gracious as we discuss the Bible. There is room for discussion and exploration—in fact, it glorifies God when we humbly and patiently examine the Bible together. The point is simply this: take God's words at face value and do what He tells you to do.

5. *Do you have a tendency to interpret the Bible allegorically or figuratively? If so, why do you think you tend to do this?*

Study the Grammatical Context

As we have seen, God used human language to write the Bible. He led human authors to use human words and human grammar in order to record His truth. So it only makes sense to pay attention to the grammar of the Bible. This doesn't mean that you need to be a grammatical expert to read the Bible (though God does give these people to the church to guide the rest of us), but we should pay attention to how the words in the Bible are being used.

The biblical authors often pay very close attention to grammar. To give one example, Paul made a significant theological point based on the use of a singular noun (rather than a plural) in Genesis 12:

> Now the promises were made to Abraham and to
> his offspring. It does not say, "And to offsprings,"
> referring to many, but referring to one, "And to
> your offspring," who is Christ. (Gal. 3:16)

This doesn't mean that we will always find interpretive gems by examining the grammar, but when we come to difficult passages, we will want to ask questions like the following:

- Who is doing the action here? (Find the subject)
- What action is the actor performing? (Find the verb)
- How are the actor and the action described? (Find the adjectives and adverbs)
- Who or what is being acted upon? (Find the direct and indirect objects)

Most of the time, we do this sort of analysis automatically, without even thinking about what we're doing. (You just did it with the previous sentence, and now you're doing it again.) But when you encounter a passage that seems difficult, try breaking it down and examining what is really going on with each sentence. God's words are worth evaluating at this level.

Study the Historical Context

The historical setting of a passage will often shed light on what the passage means. Sometimes this will require outside resources, like a study Bible, Bible dictionary, or commentary. But many times the historical insights can be found in the Bible itself. For example, much of the Old Testament consists of detailed historical accounts. And many New Testament books give historical insights—particularly the Gospels and the book of Acts.

Consider just one example of how the historical setting can help us understand the Bible. Walk into any Christian bookstore and you will find decorative knick-knacks bearing Jeremiah 29:11: "For I know the plans I have for you, declares the LORD, plans for welfare and not for evil, to give you a future and a hope." People love it because they interpret it as God saying He will keep us from harm and bless us. But is that really what Jeremiah intended to communicate to us?

If we look at the historical context, we find that Jeremiah was writing to Jewish exiles in Babylon. They had gone into captivity as punishment for their lack of faithfulness to God. Jeremiah told them that they would be in captivity for seventy years, so they should settle in and seek to bless Babylon while they were there. And then comes Jeremiah 29:11. God promised that He did indeed have a plan for His people, and He would restore them to the land of Israel after their days of exile were over.

The historical context reveals that Jeremiah 29:11 is not a blank-check promise from God that nothing bad will ever happen to any of us today. We have much to learn from God's provision for Israel in the midst of their exile and punishment. We can even make observations about God's compassion in this story and trust that this same compassionate God will care for us today. But we would be misusing Scripture if we assumed that those words could be directly applied to every circumstance as a promise of prosperity. The historical context does not always affect the meaning of a passage, but we must always consider who the biblical authors were addressing and why.

6. *In your own words, explain why paying attention to the grammatical and historical context is important. How should these concepts shape your study of the Bible?*

Let Go of Your Baggage

As important as it is to pay attention to the context of the passages we read, the greatest danger in biblical interpretation comes from our own "baggage." For example, many Americans assume that Jesus is a white, blond-haired, blue-eyed capitalist who bleeds red, white, and blue. But that is simply not the case. We often assume that God wants us to be happy, healthy, and fulfilled because that's the message we get from everyone around us. But again, that's not the case. Read the Bible carefully and you'll see that God doesn't necessarily want those things for us, at least not in the way our culture defines and pursues them.

Life experiences can also taint the way we read the Bible. Those abandoned or abused by their fathers may struggle more to understand what the Bible says about our loving heavenly Father. Those who were raised with few rules and weak parents may have a hard time seeing the power and sovereignty of God. Our experiences have an impact on our desires, which in turn affect our interpretations.

When we read the Bible, we need to do everything we can to avoid making assumptions about what the Bible is saying. We need to let it speak for itself. We are all tainted by the commitments and assumptions of our culture. We also have been heavily affected by our life experiences, but the more we let go of our baggage and ask God to speak directly to us through His Word, the more we will find God's truth transforming our minds and actions, and the better we will understand the mind of God.

7. *What would it mean for you to read the Bible with an awareness of your own baggage and a willingness to get rid of those assumptions for the sake of understanding God's truth more clearly?*

A Note on Application

Don't forget what you read in the session. Accurately interpreting the Bible is not the final step. The purpose of reading and interpreting the Bible is obedience and fellowship with God. If we interpret Scripture perfectly, yet fail to live in accordance with what we read, we are fooling ourselves (James 1:22). God has given us the precious gift of the Bible so that we will be transformed by its truth, becoming more like Him and growing in our love for Him.

8. *In light of what you have thought through in this session, how do you need to change your approach to reading and studying the Bible?*

   Watch the video for this session at multiplymovement.com.

Part IV: Understanding the Old Testament

1: Creation

Setting the Stage

The Bible tells a story. We tend to view the Bible as a bunch of fragmented bits of history, poetry, and moral tales, but in reality, the Bible tells a story. And it's a *true* story. It's a story that gives meaning to our existence, our daily lives, and to every other story on earth.

As you read through the Bible, pay attention to the story that is unfolding. But don't imagine that you're merely looking into the past when you read this story. This is a story that has yet to be finished. Though Revelation ties up the loose ends and tells us how the story will come to a close, we're not there yet. The story continues, and each and every one of us has a role to play. But we won't be able to play our part until we buy into the story so deeply that it shapes everything about our lives.

Ultimately, this is a story about God, the world He created, and the incredible plan of redemption that unfolds as He creates a people for His own glory. As you walk through key points in the biblical story over the weeks ahead, make sure you place yourself within this story. How do the actions, events, and truths presented in the story touch your life? How should you live now in light of this amazing story?

The passage you will consider in this session (Genesis 1–2) sets the stage for the rest of the Bible. In this section, we see the world as it should be. We see God crafting a world that is everything He desires it to be—no sin, no imperfection, everything glorifies God perfectly. Understanding this first part of the story will help us understand everything that follows.

1. *Read Genesis 1–2. As you read, look for elements that will help orient you to the biblical story. Who are we introduced to in this section? What is being emphasized? What seems to be the point? After reading these two chapters, make some notes below.*

Who Is God?

The story begins with familiar words: "In the beginning, God created the heavens and the earth." With these words we are introduced to the most important character in the story. It's interesting that although these are the first words in the entire Bible, the author doesn't pause to tell us theologically or philosophically who God is. There are many questions that we could ask at this point: Where did

God come from? What was He doing before He created? Why is He creating in the first place?

But Genesis proceeds in a different manner. The author teaches us about God by simply telling us what He did: He created. We're going to find out so much more about God as the story unfolds, and at points we will get specific theological answers to some of the questions we may have. But it's important to let the story drive our understanding of who God is.

2. Take a minute to reflect on what you read in Genesis 1–2. What do God's actions in this passage reveal about who He is?

This Is God's World

Perhaps the most obvious thing that we see in this passage is God's absolute power and unrivaled glory. The story starts with Him alone. There is great significance to the fact that God is the only character in Genesis 1. He is the only eternal person or thing in the universe. This means that nothing else can be equated or even compared with Him.

Allow yourself to feel the weight of this for a minute. There was a time when our universe did not exist. Immediately before our world began, God existed—and that's it! Then God began creating our world out of nothing simply by speaking. He told land to form and it obeyed. He called light into being and it happened. Every single thing in our universe came into existence in obedience to God's command.

Try to get a feel for the absolute difference between this all-powerful God who has always existed and the creation that He called forth through the repeated refrain: "Let there be _____." There is no person, force, or thing that can compete with God or claim any importance in comparison with Him. It is this absolute distinction between God and everything else that leads the angels in heaven to cry out, "Holy! Holy! Holy!"

3. *How should God's eternality and power in the creation account affect the way we view and relate to Him?*

We cannot read Genesis 1–2 without realizing that this world belongs to God. If we were to begin with our own perception of the world, we might get the sense that the world belongs to us, that we are the rightful rulers of this planet. But Genesis tells a different story. God lovingly and powerfully created this world. No person or thing had any place in this world until God put it in its proper place. God alone can claim ownership of this world because He spoke it into existence.

This should lead us to great humility about our place in this world. We are not the center of the universe. God created this world and graciously placed us in the midst of it. But all ownership and authority belongs to God. As we will see, God does delegate a certain authority to us, but this is a derived authority, graciously given to us by God to be used in a specific manner. Any attempt to claim power for ourselves independent of God is like a clay pot challenging the authority of the potter who formed it. (This is an image, by the way, which Scripture uses to describe the foolishness of challenging God—see Is. 29:15–16, 45:9–10, and Rom. 9:19–24.)

4. *How should God's power, authority, and ownership affect the way we view our place in this world?*

In the Image of God

After creating every detail of every aspect of the universe in which we live, God looked at everything He had made and declared it good. But in the midst of this episode of creation, God paused to confer with Himself:

> Then God said, "Let us make man in our image, after our likeness. And let them have dominion over the fish of the sea and over the birds of the heavens and over the livestock and over all the earth

and over every creeping thing that creeps on the earth"
(Gen. 1:26).

There is something absolutely unique about humanity. On the
one hand, we are utterly unlike God because, just like everything else
in creation, He made us. But on the other hand, *God specifically created us to be like Him*. This is impossible to wrap our minds around,
but God created us like Him in some respect and then set us in the
midst of this world to represent Him!

There is a lot of debate about what exactly the "image of God" is.
Everyone seems to agree that being created in God's image is more than
a physical resemblance—He is *Spirit*, after all (John 4:24). Suggestions
as to what God's image in humanity consists of are varied: our ability
to reason, our ability to make moral decisions, our personalities, and
our capacity for relationships are all leading views. Others suggest that
the image of God relates to the dominion over the rest of creation that
God gave to man (this ties Gen. 1:26–27 to Gen. 1:28).

Perhaps it is best not to attach the image of God to any one
faculty or attribute of humanity. In the New Testament, we are told
that Jesus Christ is "the image of the invisible God" (Col. 1:15).
Jesus is said to be "the radiance of the glory of God and the exact
imprint of his nature" (Heb. 1:3). It seems that being the "image of
God" is about reflecting God in some way. Jesus did this perfectly,
but humanity has also been given a responsibility to show God to
the world—His handiwork, nature, and attributes are displayed in
us in a way that they are not displayed in the rest of the creation.
(Of course, this image has been tainted by sin, but that comes later
in the story.)

In the ancient world, kings would set up an image of themselves as a visual announcement of who was in charge. It reminded the king's own people and the surrounding nations that this land was under the king's jurisdiction and authority. Psalm 8 says that God placed human beings in a privileged position amid the universe He created—it says we are "crowned with glory and honor" and that we have been given dominion over the works of God's hands (v. 5). It seems that God made people to humbly and graciously mediate His rule on the earth. Human beings stand as a reminder that God is the King of this world.

So rather than trying to identify the image of God with a specific aspect of the human condition, perhaps we should simply acknowledge that God made us to reflect Him to the world. We represent to the world its rightful King and we illustrate His workmanship, attributes, and characteristics.

5. *In your own words, describe why it is significant that God created us "in His image." How should this affect the way we view ourselves and the people around us?*

The Personal God of Genesis 2

Something interesting happens when we move from Genesis 1 into Genesis 2. In chapter 1, God is referred to by the title "Elohim," which simply means "God." It's a lot like referring to a person based on his or her title: "Doctor, Professor, President, King," etc. But when we get to chapter 2, the name for God changes. Now He is referred to as "Yahweh Elohim," which combines the title "God" with a personal name: Yahweh. (For good but complicated reasons, most English translations render *Yahweh* as *the* LORD (notice it's in all caps).)

This is significant because God tends to use His personal name, Yahweh, when He is relating to His people in a personal way. God uses the name Yahweh when He enters into a covenant with His people. When God makes a covenant, He specifies what His relationship to His people will look like, makes them promises, and often charges them to be obedient in return. The personal name Yahweh is appropriate for this type of interaction.

Genesis 2 is a much more intimate account of the world's origins than Genesis 1. Whereas Genesis 1 gives a broad overview of how the world was made, Genesis 2 takes that account for granted and tells the story in a much more specific way. It tells the story of humanity—created in God's own image—and the privileges and responsibilities that God gave them.

We see God doing something unique with humanity. God first formed Adam out of the ground, then bent down and breathed life into his nostrils. This is a much more intimate form of creation than we saw in chapter 1, where God simply spoke the world into existence. Notice also that God spoke directly with the man in chapter 2. He told Adam about the garden—in particular, He told Adam what he could and could not eat. Right away we see that humanity was made to communicate with God. Even in his perfect state (before sin entered the world), Adam was dependent on revelation from God in order to live in the world that God made.

And then notice that God did not want the man to be alone. This is the first time that God said something was "not good." He created a "helper fit for Adam." It's easy to imagine God enjoying His relationship with Adam and lovingly watching Adam enjoy the perfect companion that God made for him. While it is important to see the implications for marriage inherent in this passage, we should also see that God did not want man to live in isolation. God solved Adam's loneliness by creating a wife for him, but keep in mind that Eve was not just a wife—she was another human being. In other words, God designed human beings to live in relationship with other human beings. This will have major implications when we begin discussing the concept of the church in the New Testament.

6. *What can we learn about human beings and their relationship with God and each other by reading Genesis 2?*

Life in the Garden

Genesis 1–2 also gives us an amazing vision of what God originally intended the world to be. After creating the earth and everything in it, God took the time to plant a garden (2:8). God placed people in the midst of this garden and gave them the specific task of "working it and keeping it" (Gen. 2:15).

We sometimes think that work is the product of the fall, a punishment for sin. When humanity sinned, God cursed the ground, and labor became frustrating and painful (Gen. 3:17–19). But God's original intention for people was that we would be actively involved in caring for the creation. God placed Adam in the garden (keep in mind that a garden is different from a wilderness or jungle in that it is tended, planned, and ordered) and gave him the specific task of working it.

God intended for humanity to have a caring relationship with the surrounding world. God gave people dominion over the creation, placing it under their feet (Gen. 1:28 and Ps. 8:5–8), not so that they could exploit and destroy the earth, but so that they could lovingly care for it as a good creation of God meant to be protected and enjoyed.

It is also fascinating to read the account of Adam naming the animals (2:18–20). Here we get another taste of the interaction between God and humanity in a perfect world. Surely God could have named the animals on His own, but He chose to give them names by working together with Adam. At this early point in the story, it is clear that God's rule over the earth will be exercised in conjunction with His chief creation, Adam.

We cannot miss the peace, harmony, and perfect beauty described in Genesis 1–2. It gives us a picture of the world as it was meant to be. It is a world that we all long for. But this is only the beginning of the story. As we will see in the next session (and as we all know from experience), something has gone tragically wrong. But this peaceful picture where everything works in perfect harmony with everything else will reappear. The paradise that we lost will eventually be regained—surpassed even—when Jesus returns to set the world to rights.

7. *Take some time to consider the picture of the world presented in Genesis 1–2. Why is this picture so appealing? Which aspects of life in the garden of Eden should we long to see restored in our world?*

 Watch the video for this session at multiplymovement.com.

2: The Fall

You may not realize this, but you felt the result of Adam and Eve's sin today. In fact, you can't go five minutes without encountering the effects of the fall. Every aspect of God's creation has been in some way tainted or distorted by sin. Everywhere we look we see pain, rebellion, brokenness, hopelessness, despair.

Even in our own hearts, we see the influence of sin. We are in a battle, and we feel it every day. No matter how badly we want to honor God, sin screams at us from all sides, begging us to rebel against God and pursue our own desires. We struggle with temptations, and we have a hard time making sense of the things we see happening around us. Every one of us has a profound sense that the world is not now as it was intended to be.

How did we get to this point? The first two chapters of Genesis describe a wonderful existence, but the next chapter takes a dark turn. Genesis 3 describes Adam and Eve's tragic failure—their fall into sin—and the devastating impact this has had on our world.

The Story Takes a Sudden Turn

The initial chapters of Genesis paint a picture of earth as a paradise. This is the world as God intended it to be. Everything is good; there is no sin, sorrow, pain, or death. Humanity lives in perfect fellowship with God, each other, and with the creation.

But turn the page from Genesis 2 to Genesis 3 and the story takes a turn for the worse. We refer to this tragic part of the story as "the fall," and it has affected each of us to the core of our being.

As Adam and Eve joyfully cared for God's creation, the serpent (whom we later learn is Satan—see Rev. 12:9) entered the scene. In a seemingly innocent manner, he asked Eve a simple question: "Did God actually say, 'You shall not eat of any tree in the garden'?" (v. 1). God had given Adam and Eve every tree in the garden as food, and only the Tree of Knowledge of Good and Evil was off limits. But as we might expect, this was the only tree that Satan wanted Eve to think about. He wanted her to feel that God was depriving her of something. He told her that eating the forbidden fruit would open her eyes so that she would be like God. He promised her good things.

Of course, life in the garden of Eden was full of good things enjoyed through the grace and presence of God. But Satan began to promise goodness *apart from God*. With this simple twist, the world that God created to be "very good" changed dramatically.

1. *Read Genesis 3. Based on the first three chapters of Genesis, why was it such a big deal for Adam and Eve to eat from the Tree of the Knowledge of Good and Evil?*

Pay attention to a key observation from this story: Satan is subtle. He does not show up dressed in a red cape with a pitchfork saying, "I am Satan, and I am here to destroy you. Follow me." Instead, he comes to us in ways that we would not expect and offers us things that seem good. This is what he did in the garden, and he does it to us today. He deceives people by making false promises. He takes what is evil and makes it appear beautiful. He takes truth and twists it.

It is also important to notice that Satan enters the biblical scene as part of God's creation. This means that he is not all powerful. He is only alive because God gives him life. He is a deadly deceiver, but his power is infinitely less than God's power. So we shouldn't be terrified of Satan's power, but we do need to be wary of his lies and manipulation.

In the case of Adam and Eve, Satan cleverly avoided asking them to reject God outright. Instead, he offered them the knowledge of good and evil. He gave them an opportunity to be in charge, to decide for themselves the difference between good and evil. God made people to be dependent on Him (that's not a bad thing, by the way!), but from this moment on, every sin has involved men and women claiming the right to govern themselves. Sin is always a declaration of autonomy.

God had given Adam and Eve specific words to follow, but they failed to view the word of God as the supreme authority. They allowed someone else's words to carry weight. They treated God's word as a lesser authority, putting their own desires above His. Whenever we disobey His commands, we are rejecting His authority and asserting our own. We basically say, "God, You may be the author of my life, but You're not the authority in my life. I choose what I do, not You. I'm in control here, not You."

2. *Analyze the sin in your life in light of the rebellion of Adam and Eve in Genesis 3. Do you see the same tendency toward independence and rebellion in your actions? How so?*

The World Became a Different Place

From this point on, the biblical story is saturated with the effects of the fall. Suddenly people find themselves separated from God, those around them, and the creation. Whereas Adam and Eve once enjoyed perfect fellowship with God, they now hid from Him in shame and were sent as exiles out of the paradise that had been their home. They once enjoyed a perfect relationship with each another, but now their relationship was filled with shame, distrust, and blame. Adam and Eve once happily cared for the creation, but now they would experience pain in childbearing, the curse upon the ground, and the promise of toil in the work they had once enjoyed.

The effects of the fall are also known as "the curse." In response to the sin of the first human beings, God cursed (1) the serpent, (2) Eve, (3) Adam, and (4) the rest of creation. The serpent was cursed to crawl around on his belly and, along with his offspring, to live in enmity against the offspring of the woman. Eve was cursed through pain in childbearing and strife with her spouse. Adam was cursed with pain and frustration in working the ground. And on Adam's account, the rest of the creation was cursed to produce thorns and thistles, or as Paul later stated it, the creation was "subjected to futility" and was placed in "bondage to corruption" (Rom. 8:20–21). Of course the greatest consequence was death—spiritual death immediately, and physical death eventually.

Many Christians have heard the story of the fall so many times they have become anesthetized to just how tragic this event was. We don't know how long Adam and Eve lived in the garden, but they literally lived in Paradise. They inhabited a perfect world where everything and everyone did exactly what God designed them to do. They actually experienced a perfect human relationship! They enjoyed relationship with God—to the point that they would walk with Him through the garden! We are so far from this reality that it is entirely unimaginable.

But then they lost it. The action itself might appear harmless (how much harm can a piece of fruit cause?), but the outward act represented something far more sinister. The first sin was rebellion, idolatry, treason, and pride, all rolled into a single bite. Both Adam and Eve made a conscious choice to rebel against their Creator and live on their own terms. And we imitate their decision every time we choose our desires over God's.

3. *Think back to the world of Genesis 2. Spend a few minutes imagining what our world would look like without sin, if everything had stayed the way God intended it to be. Make some notes below.*

4.   *Now consider the ways that sin has affected our world. How is our
     experience of the world shaped by the fall? Be specific and describe
     how it affects you today.*

From Cain to Babel

As we keep turning pages from Genesis 3, we see the effects of sin
continuing to play themselves out. First we see Cain kill Abel. When
his brother's sacrifice pleased God and his own did not, Cain acted
in jealous passion and committed the first murder. As if this wasn't
bad enough, we immediately find Lamech writing the first poem
recorded in the Bible in order to brag about being more vengeful
than Cain. Clearly a trend has begun in the wrong direction.

In fact, sin and rebellion spread so quickly that before we get very
far into the story, God felt the need to destroy the whole world. It's
a stark reminder of the devastation that so quickly comes upon us
when we live independently of God. Genesis 6 opens with a disturbing
analysis: "The LORD saw that the wickedness of man was great in the
earth, and that every intention of the thoughts of his heart was only
evil continually" (v. 5). The creature whom God crafted into His image
to be His representative on the earth had now become so twisted that
his mind and will were described as *"only evil continually."*

Next, God punished them for their rebellion. He sent a flood that
destroyed every person on the face of the earth with the exception of

Noah and his family. God's purpose for the human race would start over through Noah and his descendants. You would think that the horror of the flood would cause Noah's descendants to live in obedience, but soon after the flood we find humanity joined together in rebellion against God.

This time people gathered together at Babel to build a tower to the heavens. Their purpose was to unite themselves in this great project and make a name for themselves. Once again, God looked down on humanity's declaration of autonomy and destroyed the fruit of their rebellion. This time He confused their language and scattered them across the face of the earth. As we come to the end of Genesis 11, humanity's ability to accurately represent God on earth—to live as His image bearers—is in serious question.

5. *Think about the current state of the world. In what ways is humanity still caught in the rebellion that led to the flood and the tower of Babel?*

6. *In what ways are you involved in this rebellion?*

The Story Continues in Spite of Sin

Thankfully, the biblical story does not end with Genesis 11! We need to understand that the Bible could have stopped at Genesis 11, and God would have been completely fair and loving to end the human race right there. But in His perfect wisdom, God kept the story in motion. Now the stage was set for God's plan of redemption. God gave humanity a responsibility, but they completely failed, and now they needed someone to redeem them.

Even in these early stages of the story, we see snapshots of God's willingness to rescue and redeem. Immediately after Adam and Eve rebelled against God, we read God's promise in Genesis 3:15 that there will be enmity between the serpent and the woman, and between the serpent's offspring and the woman's offspring. God says, "He shall bruise your head, and you shall bruise his heel." This imagery is a picture of a forthcoming battle between Christ and the serpent, and we are guaranteed that the serpent will be crushed. When we arrive in the New Testament, we find Paul encouraging Christians in Rome by promising that, "The God of peace will soon crush Satan under your feet" (Rom. 16:20).

We receive even more hope when God makes a covenant with Noah (Gen. 6:18, 9:9). A covenant is a promise from God, an agreement between God and His people that He will bless them in accordance with certain terms. As the story unfolds, we see God establishing a people through covenants. These covenants play a major role in how God relates to His people. With Noah, the covenant was about saving a people for Himself. Amid all of the people who would justly experience His judgment, God made a covenant with Noah. He called out a people by His grace and promised to preserve His creation.

The plan will continue to unfold as we continue in the biblical story, but Genesis 1–11 lays the groundwork and orients us to what is coming.

7. *As you think back over Genesis 1–3 (and even the events we discussed from chapters 4–11), briefly describe how these chapters lay the groundwork for what is to come in the biblical story.*

8. *How should our understanding of the first chapters of the Bible affect the way we view ourselves and the world around us?*

 Watch the video for this session at multiplymovement.com.

3: God's Covenant with Abraham

Though we are still at the beginning of the biblical storyline, a pattern has already developed: People sin, people face the consequences, God redeems. People sin, people face the consequences, God redeems.

As we saw in the previous session, when Adam and Eve sinned, God cursed the earth and then told Eve that her descendant would crush the head of the serpent (Gen. 3:15)—a promise that Jesus will one day destroy Satan and his works (Rom. 16:20). Only a few chapters later, we find people sinning continually, to the point that God destroyed all but eight humans by flooding the earth. But as soon as the waters subsided, God made a covenant with Noah, promising, "I will never again curse the ground because of man, for the intention of man's heart is evil from his youth. Neither will I ever again strike down every living creature as I have done" (Gen. 8:21). People sin, people face the consequences, God redeems.

Once again, in Genesis 11, the human race gathered at Babel in defiance of God in order to "make a name for themselves." God's response was to confuse their speech and divide them. But just when we think that humanity has no hope, God launched a plan of redemption that was global: to create a people for Himself who would embody and spread His salvation to every group of people on the planet. After cursing and scattering humanity, God made a promise to bless all of the nations. And God set this plan in motion by calling one man living in the middle of an idol-worshipping nation away from everything he once knew. And He promised to change the course of history through this man and his offspring.

God's Promise of Redemption

God's plan to rescue the world from sin started very quietly. God chose one man, Abraham, and said:

> Go from your country and your kindred and your father's house to the land that I will show you. And I will make of you a great nation, and I will bless you and make your name great, so that you will be a blessing. I will bless those who bless you, and him who dishonors you I will curse, and in you all the families of the earth shall be blessed. (Gen. 12:1–3)

It may not sound like much, but with these words God put into motion a plan that would lead Paul to cry out in amazement about "the depth of the riches and wisdom and knowledge of God" (Rom. 11:33). This plan would eventually reach its climax in Jesus's incarnation, death, and resurrection—events that took place at "the fullness of time" (Gal. 4:4). In other words, human history was working toward this moment, the central point in God's plan of righting what went wrong with the fall.

As soon as sin entered the world, God began to reveal His plan to reverse the effects of the fall. He would restore us and the world around us to what He originally created—and more. God made a promise to Adam and Eve, then to Noah, and here God made a covenant with Abraham. At a few key points in Abraham's life (Gen. 12:1–9; 15:1–21; 17:1–14), God spoke with Abraham and revealed more about His plan. But the basics are clear from the beginning: God promised to make Abraham into a great nation, to make his name great, and to bless him so that he would be a blessing to "every family of the earth."

1. *Take some time to read and meditate on Genesis 12:1–9, 15:1–21, and 17:1–14. What stands out to you from reading the promises that God gave to Abraham?*

2. *What does God's covenant with Abraham reveal to us about God?*

3. *What does God's covenant with Abraham reveal about God's plan of*
    redemption?

4. *Consider the biblical pattern: people sin, people suffer the consequences,*
    God redeems. How have you seen this pattern in your own life?

The Covenant Confirmed

Land was an important part of God's promise to Abraham. God's
initial call to Abraham involved leaving his own land and going
to the land that God called him to (12:1), a land that God would
promise to give to Abraham and his offspring (12:7; 15:7, 18–20).
God was going to establish His people in the land of Canaan, the
"promised land." It would belong to Abraham and his descendants.
In many ways, the rest of the Old Testament (and much of subse-
quent history) revolves around this land.

When God promised to give this land to Abraham, Abraham
asked, "How am I to know that I shall possess it?" God's answer

to Abraham was to confirm His covenant by walking in between the separated halves of dead (sacrificed) animals (Gen. 15:9–17). Around the time of Abraham, covenant agreements often took this form, where the parties involved in a covenant would walk between animals that had been sacrificed. By doing this, each person was essentially saying, "If I break my word in this covenant, may I be cursed like this dead animal."

In the case of His covenant with Abraham, God caused Abraham to fall asleep, and then He came down in the image of a smoking firepot and flaming torch and walked through the separated halves of the sacrificed animals by Himself. This gives us a picture of God's commitment to His people. For one thing, it's incredible to think that God would come down and make an agreement with a mere man. But it's also amazing that God put Abraham to sleep while He walked through the animal pieces alone. He seems to have been showing that He was committed to keeping the covenant regardless of whether Abraham and His offspring were faithful to keep it or not. Theologians call this a unilateral covenant. God made this promise to bless Abraham and to use him to bless the world. This was God's decision, and He will uphold the covenant no matter what happens.

5. *In Genesis 15, God made it clear that His promises to Abraham were not dependent on Abraham. How should this affect the way we think about God's plan of redemption?*

Creating a People for Himself

We might have expected God to rescue the world through some loud and dramatic event. But it all started very subtly. God began to unfold His plan with a promise. But it isn't a small promise. It's a promise with huge implications. The entire plan of redemption that unfolds in the rest of the Bible is God's fulfilling His promises to Abraham. Literally, all of world history is related to the promises that God made to Abraham. God would make a great nation out of Abraham and his wife Sarah, and through that nation He would re-form creation and transform the nations.

God's covenant with Abraham signaled the introduction of what would become known as the people of Israel, the covenant people of God in the Old Testament. In Genesis 17:7–8 God began using language that gets repeated throughout the Old Testament in the phrase: "I will be your God and you will be my people." First of all, don't miss the crux of this promise. God was offering the greatest blessing He could give anyone: Himself. He promised to be their God! We often forget what an honor it is that God would offer relationship. We can get so accustomed to people begging us to follow God that we forget what a miracle it is that we are invited. In making this covenant with Abraham, God made the tremendous offer of being his God and the God of his offspring. Here God was creating a people for Himself. In a special sense, God would belong to this people, and this people would belong to Him.

When we studied creation, we noted that because we are created in the image of God, we have a responsibility to reflect God to the world around us. By the time of Abraham, humanity had generally failed in this. But through Abraham and his descendants, God was forming a people who would embody God's intention for humanity. They would live in a close relationship with God and reflect Him to the world around them. With His promise to make a great nation for Abraham and to bless all the nations through Him, God was once again commissioning humanity to live as His representatives on earth.

6. *In your own words, explain why it is significant that God created a people for Himself. What did God want to accomplish through this "great nation" He promised to form?*

The Gospel According to Abraham

It would be difficult for us to overestimate the importance of God's covenant with Abraham. God was defining what His relationship with fallen humanity would look like and announcing His plan to bless the world. What we see in God's promise to Abraham is nothing short of the gospel itself. Paul said:

> Know then that it is those of faith who are the sons of Abraham. And the Scripture, foreseeing that God would justify the Gentiles by faith, *preached the gospel beforehand to Abraham*, saying, "In you shall all the nations be blessed." So then, those who

are of faith are blessed along with Abraham, the man
of faith. (Gal. 3:7–9)

Paul was saying that when God spoke these simple words to
Abraham, "In you shall all the nations be blessed," He was preaching the gospel. Though Abraham may not have known exactly what
this blessing for all the nations would entail, He took God at His
word (at least at this moment in his life) and trusted in what God
would do.

From the very beginning, God called Abraham's descendants,
the people of Israel, to be a blessing to the nations. But as we will
see as we study the rest of the Old Testament, they never really rose
to that task. In fact, the nations were not fully blessed through
Abraham until Jesus Christ, the ultimate descendant of Abraham,
arrived. Jesus identified Himself as the fulfillment of this promise to
Abraham: "Your father Abraham rejoiced that he would see my day.
He saw it and was glad" (John 8:56). With Jesus, we finally see all
the nations being blessed as they are called to join the people of God.

7. *Consider God's intentions to bless "all the nations" through His
   promise to Abraham. What implications does this have for the way
   we view the world today?*

God told Abraham, "I will bless you and make your name great, so that you will be a blessing" (Gen. 12:2). Don't miss this principle: God's blessings are meant to be shared, not hoarded. In blessing Abraham, God was intentionally seeking to bless the world. This is much different from the way most Christians view their blessings. We tend to think that God blesses us so that we can be happy, comfortable, secure, etc. We live as though our blessings were meant for us alone. But God's blessing for Abraham shows us God's plans in blessing us. When we receive God's blessings, we should immediately look around us to see whom we can bless.

8. *Think about the ways that God has blessed you. How should these blessings be used to benefit the people around you?*

The Faith of Abraham

The New Testament makes a big deal out of the faith of Abraham. And rightly so. In Genesis 15, Abraham stood before God and voiced his confusion over God's promise to make him into a great nation. Abraham said to God, "You've made these promises [back in Genesis 12], but I have absolutely no offspring. I have only a servant in my household to be my heir." God responded by bringing him outside and telling him to look toward the heavens and count the stars, if he was able to number them. And then God said, "So shall your offspring be."

And what did Abraham say in response to this? Nothing. Genesis 15 doesn't record a single word from Abraham in response. It seems that he was speechless. But the Bible does tell us one important thing about Abraham's response: Abraham believed God. God made a huge promise that seemed impossible, and Abraham simply took God at His word. He believed it would happen just as God said. And then Genesis 15 adds a very significant comment: "He believed the LORD, and He counted it to him as righteousness" (v. 6). His simple belief in God's promise was "credited to him" as righteousness. He was declared to be in a right relationship with God because of his faith.

Romans 4 adds an incredible commentary on this statement and applies it to those of us who follow Jesus today:

> The words "it was counted to him" were not written for his sake alone, but for ours also. It will be counted to us who believe in him who raised from the dead Jesus our Lord, who was delivered up for our trespasses and raised for our justification. (vv. 23–25)

Paul was saying that Genesis 15:6 was written down for our sake so that we would believe in the Jesus who died to pay for our sins and the God who raised Him from the dead. Abraham lived some four thousand years before Jesus came to the earth, but he was declared righteous because he believed what God said about what He would do through Abraham's descendant, Jesus Christ. We live some two thousand years after Jesus came to the earth, but we are declared righteous when we believe what God says about what He has done through Abraham's descendant, Jesus Christ.

Through Abraham, God set into motion His plan to redeem the world by creating a people for Himself. And ultimately He would send His Son Jesus Christ, Abraham's descendant, to set the world to rights. We will discuss Jesus much more in future sessions, but for now, it's important to see the plan as it develops with Abraham.

9. *Read Romans 4. Why do you think the New Testament makes such a big deal about Abraham's faith?*

10. *How should Abraham's faith affect the way you think about and relate to God?*

11. *Spend some time in prayer. Ask God to increase your faith in Him. Ask Him to make you more consistently aware of His plan of redemption and the role He wants you to play in that.*

 Watch the video for this session at multiplymovement.com.

4: Exodus and Redemption

As we turn the last pages of Genesis, we see God working toward the fulfillment of His promises to Abraham. God's people had grown significantly, which was perfectly in line with His promise that Abraham's descendants would be "as numerous as the stars in the sky." But as soon as we start reading in the book of Exodus, it looks like something has gone wrong. Exodus begins with a significant problem: God's people are slaves in a foreign land.

Israel's Captivity

Understand that the first two chapters of Exodus cover four hundred years. We can quickly read over descriptions of the Israelites[1] making

---

1   The "Israelites" are the descendants of Abraham. They are named after
     Jacob (Abraham's grandson), whose name God changed to "Israel."

Pharaoh's[2] bricks and building Pharaoh's cities, yet overlook the fact that this had been going on for a long time! These short stories summarize a huge amount of suffering. Understandably, the Israelites seem to have given up hope by this point—after all, they were forced to continue in backbreaking labor day after day, generation after generation, without any indication that it would end.

This raises an important question: Was God really keeping His promises to Abraham if his descendants were slaves in Egypt? The answer is yes. In fact, God specifically told Abraham that this would happen:

> The LORD said to Abram, "Know for certain that your offspring will be sojourners in a land that is not theirs and will be servants there, and they will be afflicted for four hundred years. But I will bring judgment on the nation that they serve, and afterward they shall come out with great possessions."
> (Gen. 15:13–14)

God's promises to Abraham were exactly on track, and as the book of Exodus opens, the scene is being set for the greatest act of redemption that the world has seen to this point. Here we find God's people in an impossible situation without any hope of relief. If God is going to keep His promises to Abraham, then He will have to accomplish something spectacular. As it turns out, God's display of power in Israel's exodus is frequently mentioned in the rest of the

---

2   "Pharaoh" was the title of the ruler of Egypt.

Bible as clear evidence of God's commitment to His people and His power to redeem.

Moses's Encounter with I AM

Adding to the agony of slavery, Pharaoh commanded that all male Hebrew babies were to be drowned in the Nile River. It is at this seemingly hopeless time that we meet Moses. By his mother's cunning and God's provision, Moses survived this slaughter. At this vulnerable moment at the beginning of his life, no one could have predicted how greatly God would use Moses.

After Moses's mother saved him by floating him down the Nile in a basket, Pharaoh's daughter discovered, raised, and educated him. Though trained in the house of Pharaoh, it seems that Moses deeply understood his connection to the nation of Israel. In fact, it was an early attempt to fight for his people by murdering an Egyptian that led Moses to flee to the wilderness.

During this period of exile, God was preparing to rescue His people from slavery:

> During those many days the king of Egypt died, and the people of Israel groaned because of their slavery and cried out for help. Their cry for rescue from slavery came up to God. And God heard their groaning, and God remembered his covenant with Abraham, with Isaac, and with Jacob. God saw the people of Israel—and God knew. (Ex. 2:23–25)

It is important to recognize that what God was about to do here was directly related to His covenant with Abraham. Though the situation seemed entirely hopeless, God "saw" His people, and He "knew."

Just as He did with Abraham, God chose to begin this next phase of redemptive history through one man: Moses. As Moses tended his father-in-law's sheep in the wilderness, Moses had an unforgettable encounter with God—an event that changed his life and shapes our understanding of who God is.

1. *Read Exodus 2:23–3:22 carefully. It records one of the rare instances when a human being had an audible conversation with Almighty God. What stands out to you about Moses's encounter with God in this passage?*

When Moses saw the burning bush, he walked closer to see what was going on. As he approached, He heard the voice of God telling him to take off his sandals because he was standing on holy ground. As God revealed His plan to use Moses to set Israel free, Moses asked God two questions.

The first question was "Who am I?" Who am I, God, that You would send me, a stammering shepherd, to defy a powerful king and lead Your people? The second question was, "Who are You?" When people ask who sent me, what should I tell them?

Though Moses was backpedaling from what God was calling him to do, these are both excellent questions. They are the most fundamental questions we could ever ask, because everything in our lives—not only here and now, but for all of eternity—is based on a right answer to those two questions: Who am I, and who is God?

God answered Moses's first question by pointing to Himself. Moses asked, "Who am I?" and God simply replied, "I will be with you." God's response at this point should be fundamental to the way we view ourselves. From the very beginning, God's people are known as those whose God is with them. We belong to Him, and there is no way that we can define ourselves apart from God. It is His presence with us that enables us to accomplish the tasks He gives us.

In response to Moses's second question ("Who are You?"), God said very simply, "I AM WHO I AM." This is not a dismissive statement. It is very significant, and there's much to be learned from this declaration. God was explaining that He cannot define Himself by pointing to anyone or anything else. The name I AM speaks of His eternality. Whereas an appropriate name to describe us would be "I became" or "I was brought into existence," God's name is "I AM" because He has always existed. He is who He is, and that is who He will always be. This is a statement of absolute being, absolute power, absolute importance. God is who He is, and He never changes.

When we examined the creation account, we briefly looked at God's personal name in Genesis 2. That name is "Yahweh" (translated in most English Bibles as "the LORD," with all capital letters), a name that comes from this statement to Moses. "Yahweh" carries the significance of God's statement to Moses: I AM WHO I AM. The name "Yahweh" is actually used over six thousand times in the

Old Testament—three times as often as the simple name for God, "Elohim" (which is the title for God we saw in Genesis 1). The implication of this frequent use of God's personal name is that God aims to be known in Scripture not just as a generic deity, but as a specific person with a wholly unique character and a special relationship with His people.

It's impossible to convey exactly what this encounter must have been like for Moses. He walked away from his sheep because he saw something remarkable—a bush that was burning without being consumed—but he had no idea that he was actually walking into the presence of the living God. God immediately commanded Moses to take off his sandals because he was standing on holy ground. As soon as Moses saw what was really happening, he hid his face. God's holiness was more than he could bear. All he could do was listen and obey.

Let My People Go

God then sent Moses back to Egypt to lead His people out of slavery and into the land that He had promised to give Abraham's descendants. When Moses arrived, he gave Pharaoh a simple command from God: "Let my people go!"

Not only did Pharaoh refuse to let Israel go free, he intensified their labor to the point that the Israelites got angry at Moses for provoking Pharaoh. Even Moses himself seemed to have lost heart at this point. But God continued to carry out His plan of redemption, showing His resolve to keep His covenant with Abraham and to free His people from bondage.

2. *Read Exodus 5:22–6:13. What does this passage reveal about God and His relationship to His people?*

Understand that this battle is nothing short of a showdown between Yahweh, the God of Israel, and Pharaoh, the supposed son of the sun god, Ra. The Egyptians earnestly believed that their king was a god, and as such, he was responsible for maintaining order in the natural world. When God used Moses to deliver the ten plagues, He was demonstrating His absolute power over everything that Egypt's god-king claimed control over. Many of the plagues seem to have been directed against specific Egyptian deities (e.g., the plague of darkness would have been an embarrassment to Ra, the sun god), but all of them would have undermined Pharaoh's claim to deity.

Just as we saw in the accounts of creation, the flood, and the tower of Babel, we are seeing that God controls every aspect of the world He created, and He will not share His authority with anyone. He fights for His own glory and proves that He is the ultimate power and only true God.

The Passover Lamb

Though God clearly demonstrated His power over Pharaoh and all of Egypt's gods through the first nine plagues, it was the tenth plague that ultimately got Pharaoh's attention. God warned that unless Pharaoh released His people, every firstborn in the land of Egypt would be killed. Tragically, Pharaoh refused, and the consequences were devastating:

> At midnight the LORD struck down all the firstborn in the land of Egypt, from the firstborn of Pharaoh who sat on his throne to the firstborn of the captive who was in the dungeon, and all the firstborn of the livestock. And Pharaoh rose up in the night, he and all his servants and all the Egyptians. And there was a great cry in Egypt, for there was not a house where someone was not dead. (Ex. 12:29–30)

It is difficult to image such a scene. It is morbid and hard to stomach, but it teaches us an important lesson about God. Just as He is faithful to keep His promises of blessing, God is also faithful to carry out His warnings of wrath. This is important to keep in mind in a time when so many doubt and even ridicule God's intention to punish.

Notice that God had graciously offered the Egyptians an alternative before it got to this point. Pharaoh could have submitted to God's call and his nation would have been preserved. God also provided an alternative for the Israelites. Any Israelite who put the blood of a lamb on their doorpost would be "passed over"—the angel of death would move on to the next house.

Imagine what this would have been like for the Israelites. Imagine bringing a cute lamb into your house, a lamb that you and your kids feed, care for, and play with. And then, just when your kids are getting used to this nice little lamb, you slaughter it. You take its blood, and as your children watch, you wipe it across the doorpost over your home. That's an image that sticks with a kid—and a family.

And imagine your little boy or your little girl asking, "Why did you do that, Daddy?" And your response would be: "The lamb was a substitute. Instead of someone in our family dying, the lamb died. Look at your brother, and realize that the lamb died instead of him."

The stark reality of that night is that the only people who were exempt from judgment were those who put blood on their doorposts, and in so doing, trusted that death would pass over them. It's not that the Israelites didn't experience God's judgment because they were better people. They escaped God's judgment simply because they trusted in the sacrifice provided by God. And everyone—even slaves—who trusted in that sacrifice was spared on that night.

This is the picture we see throughout Scripture, and it is important to keep in mind for the next session when you read about God's covenant with Moses and the laws that God gave to govern His people. Keep in mind that from the very beginning the only way to receive forgiveness was through trusting the Forgiver. The only way to be a recipient of the promises of God is to trust God. The people were saved only because they trusted God as they saw the blood of a spotless lamb over their doorposts.

This night was the first Passover, an event that the Jews have celebrated once a year ever since. It is full of significance that Jesus, on the night He was betrayed, recast the Passover celebration in terms of His own death and resurrection. Jesus could hardly have been clearer that He was laying down His life for His followers, as their Passover Lamb.

Paul makes this connection explicit in the New Testament where he told us, "Christ, our Passover lamb, has been sacrificed" (1 Cor. 5:7).

3. *How does God's provision of the Passover Lamb for the Israelites help us understand Jesus's sacrifice for us?*

Through the Red Sea

Though the death of every firstborn in Egypt convinced Pharaoh to release the Israelites, he soon changed his mind and chased after them. This provided the backdrop for one the most memorable events in salvation history. As Israel sat with their backs to the Red Sea, Pharaoh's army approached rapidly. It seemed certain that their exodus from slavery was over immediately after it began.

But nothing is too difficult for God; nothing can stop Him from fulfilling His promises. He proved this by splitting the waters of the Red Sea, allowing His people to walk across on dry land, and then destroying Pharaoh and his army as the waters closed in around them. As God redeemed His people by leading them out of slavery, He demonstrated in dramatic fashion that Israel's God is unlike any other so-called god.

4. *Read Exodus 15:1–21. How did the Israelites describe God's act of redemption immediately after He led them out of slavery?*

Take a minute to consider the exodus account. Though God sometimes makes direct statements about who He is and how we should
relate to Him, He often reveals Himself to us through His actions.
Reflect on what God did as He called His people out of Egypt and
answer the questions below.

5.   *What do God's actions in Israel's exodus teach us about God?*

6.   *The story of the exodus sets the paradigm for what God's redemption
     looks like. How have you seen God's hand at work in your own life?*

A Forgetful People

As we close this session, it may be helpful to take note of Israel's
long-term reaction to God's incredible deliverance. What did they
do, time and again, in response to God's redemptive grace? They
forgot! They complained! They longed for the days when they were
back in Egypt.

As we read these accounts, it seems unbelievable. How could this people who had so clearly seen God's hand at work stop trusting God and begin complaining about their circumstances?

But before we become too critical of the Israelites, let's look at our own lives. We may not have been saved from an oncoming army by walking through the sea on dry land, but those events are a part of our heritage. Not only that, but we have seen God come through for us in incredibly powerful and personal ways. No matter what we try to make ourselves believe in our darkest moments, every one of us has unmistakably seen the hand of God in our lives. But we forget. We complain. We lose our trust in God and try to go back to doing things our own way.

Take some time to learn from Israel's example and focus on remembering God's provision in life's most difficult circumstances.

7. *What does Israel's tendency to forget God's redemption and begin complaining teach us about humanity?*

8. *Make this more personal. Take some time to write about the times that God rescued you. What can you do to keep yourself focused on who God is and what He has done?*

9. *Spend some time in prayer. Ask God to make the story of Israel's exodus vivid to you. Ask Him for the faith to believe that He will come through on His promises to you no matter how desperate the situation appears. Pray that God would help you trust Him for your salvation.*

 Watch the video for this session at multiplymovement.com.

5: God's Covenant with Moses

Try to place yourself in the shoes of the Israelites. They quickly went from being the slaves of one of the most powerful nations on earth to being set free through a series of frightening miracles. They watched as God made fools of Egypt's gods and Egypt's "divine" ruler through the ten plagues. They marched out of Egypt as their former masters showered them with gifts of gold, silver, and clothing. They witnessed the impossible as God led them along dry ground through the midst of a parted sea. They saw God single-handedly destroy the most powerful army in the region by simply unparting the sea.

Picture Israel standing on the far side of the Red Sea, having just witnessed some of the most dramatic events in history. They had just been claimed and rescued by a God whose power was clearly uncontested. After the glow of their exodus had worn off, the Israelites had to face some important questions: Who exactly is this God who rescued us and claimed us as His own? Where is He leading us and what are His intentions for us? What does it look like for us to live as the people of this God?

At the Base of Mount Sinai

As they walked away from the Red Sea into the wilderness, the Israelites did not know exactly what to expect. The first few months of their journey were filled with turmoil. The Israelites complained about lacking food and water. Then, when God miraculously provided fresh water and rained bread (manna) from heaven, they complained about the monotony of their diet. At one point they even got so upset that they wanted Moses dead. But everything changed—at least for a time—when they approached Mount Sinai.

When Israel arrived at the base of Mount Sinai, they discovered that God had chosen this place to reveal Himself to His people and enter into a covenant with them. Moses went up the mountain to meet with God, and God immediately explained His intention for Israel:

> The LORD called to him [Moses] out of the mountain, saying, "Thus you shall say to the house of Jacob, and tell the people of Israel: You yourselves have seen what I did to the Egyptians, and how I bore you on eagles' wings and brought you to myself. Now therefore, if you will indeed obey my voice and keep my covenant, you shall be my treasured possession among all peoples, for all the earth is mine; and you shall be to me a kingdom of priests

and a holy nation. These are the words that you shall
speak to the people of Israel." (Ex. 19:3–6)

Here God defined Israel. First of all, they were the people whom
God had miraculously rescued from slavery. It would be impossible
for God's people to define themselves without making reference to
God's act of redemption in their exodus. But this was not all. God
had "brought them to Himself." They were now God's "treasured
possession." God was using this moment at Mount Sinai to identify
Himself to His people and to tell them about their new identity.
They could now rest in the security of being treasured and protected
by God! It was also here that God would set the terms for how their
relationship would work.

Before they could begin this process, however, the people of
Israel had to prepare themselves:

> The LORD said to Moses, "Go to the people and
> consecrate them today and tomorrow, and let them
> wash their garments and be ready for the third day.
> For on the third day the LORD will come down on
> Mount Sinai in the sight of all the people. And you
> shall set limits for the people all around, saying,
> 'Take care not to go up into the mountain or touch
> the edge of it. Whoever touches the mountain shall
> be put to death.'" (Ex. 19:10–12)

The Israelites had to "consecrate themselves." Basically, they had
to set themselves apart for a specific purpose; they had to prepare

themselves for an encounter with God. This is what a relationship between a holy God and sinful people requires. While Moses met with God on Mount Sinai, the mountain was surrounded by smoke, lightning, and thunder. The people were not even allowed to touch the base of the mountain lest they be killed. God was doing something unique here, and He demonstrated this reality in dramatic fashion.

1. *Read Exodus 19. Explain the significance of the people's cleansing themselves and staying clear of the mountain.*

2. *How should Israel's encounter with God at Mount Sinai affect the way we view Him?*

A Holy God and Sinful People

At Sinai, God entered into a covenant with Moses and the rest of the Israelites. When God made His covenant with Abraham, He promised to make his descendants into a great nation, to give them the land of Canaan, and ultimately to bless all the nations of the earth through him. The covenant that God made with Moses built upon the covenant He made with Abraham. As they waited at the base of Mount Sinai, Israel learned that they were the great nation that God had promised to Abraham; they were the ones who would inherit the land of Canaan, and ultimately, their responsibility was to be a blessing to all the nations. The implications of this covenant were clear: the LORD would be Israel's God, and Israel would be His people.

As we might anticipate, however, there were some potential problems with a holy God binding Himself to sinful people. How could this sinless God maintain a relationship with people who were prone to rebel and do the things He hates? Israel would need to know what God expected of them and what it looked like to live as the people of God.

This is where the Old Testament Law came in. Unlike the covenant with Abraham, the covenant with Moses included an extensive code of conduct. This Law spelled out God's expectations for His people in their civil, religious, and moral lives. The Law began with the Ten Commandments, but from these ten simple laws followed more than one hundred specific laws related to all aspects of the life of the people of God. These laws were not intended to be comprehensive; they were meant to provide judiciary precedents through which Israel's judges could make wise decisions about any issue that might arise.

These laws were legally binding on the people of Israel in the Old Testament. When we read the New Testament, however, Jesus explained that He fulfilled the Old Testament Law (Matt. 5:17), and it is no longer binding on us as Christians (Rom. 6:14, Gal. 5:18). This means that we should not simply read the Law and directly apply it to our lives. At the same time, we cannot discard it or consider it meaningless. The Law gives insight into the character of God and His intention for His people.

For example, God commanded Israel to leave some of their produce in the fields and on the vines when they did their reaping and harvesting (Deut. 24:19–22). Strange as that may sound, it was God's way of making provision for the "sojourner, the fatherless, and the widow." As we read this command today, we don't need to literally leave some of the fruit on the vine when we harvest (how many of us actually harvest, anyway?). The point is, we need to provide for the poor. This command teaches us about God's character and about the way He wants His people to function in the world He created.

Another thing we learn from the Law is that God has every right to dictate to His created beings how they must act. He *can* tell people what they can or cannot eat, what they can or cannot touch, etc. He determines what is morally right and has the freedom to set boundaries on our conduct. This is an important lesson given the prevailing arrogance in our culture.

3. *Read Exodus 20:1–21. What do the Ten Commandments reveal about the character of God?*

4. *What do the Ten Commandments reveal about the way God wants humanity to live?*

Maintaining the Relationship

The Law poses some difficult theological questions for Christians today. We know that we are saved by grace and not by works. In other words, there is no way that we can earn our way to God by keeping rules and doing good deeds—we are too sinful to be sufficiently obedient, and God saves us by grace through faith. When we read the Old Testament Law, however, it appears as though God is giving the Law to Israel so that they can be made right with Him by rule-keeping and good deeds.

But there is nothing in the Law that tells the Israelites that they will receive ultimate salvation if they perfectly keep every aspect of the Law. In fact, the Law itself assumes that the Israelites will fail in keeping it—that's why the sacrificial system was included (we will discuss this more in the next session). The Law does promise blessing for obedience and a curse for disobedience (we will discuss this in a moment), but this is not the same thing as salvation by works. Even now God blesses us for obedience, and we suffer consequences when we rebel against Him.

In reality, the Law was never intended to give the Israelites a moral ladder they could climb and thereby earn God's favor by showing what good people they were. Instead, the Law was about maintaining a relationship with God. The Law solved the problem of how a holy God can bind Himself to a sinful people. It gave the people of Israel a tangible code of conduct that would allow them to faithfully live out their identity as the people of God. It taught them to relate to God and one another appropriately. We put too much strain on the Law when we try to make it into a system of salvation through good works.

5. *Explain the difference between Israel's keeping the Law in order to earn God's favor and keeping the Law in order to maintain a relationship with God.*

6. *In your own words, explain why it was important for God to give Israel the Law.*

Blessing and Curse

While the covenant with Moses was an extension of God's covenant with Abraham, there is an important difference between the two. With Abraham, the covenant was unconditional. In other words, God was making a promise to Abraham that was not dependent on Abraham's actions—God would fulfill this covenant no matter what Abraham did or didn't do. With Moses, however, God added a conditional element. God would bless Israel, bring them safely into the Promised Land, bless them in the land, and make them a blessing to the rest of the nations *if* they were faithful to observe God's Law.

God would always keep His promise to Abraham, but the promises He made at Mount Sinai to bless Israel were dependent on faithful obedience. These blessings were not dependent on Israel's sinless perfection—remember that God built a system of sacrifice, atonement, and forgiveness into the Law itself—but God required the Israelites to faithfully uphold their end of the covenant. If they did, they would be blessed and receive the promises. If they didn't, they would be cursed and taken into exile.

In the book of Deuteronomy, Israel stood at the brink of the Promised Land (many years after Israel stood at Mount Sinai) and prepared to walk in and claim the land that God was giving them. But before they entered the land, Moses gathered them together and reminded them of this covenant. Deuteronomy 28 clearly explains that if Israel would be faithful to God and keep this covenant with Him, He would bless them unimaginably. But if they rebelled and failed to keep their end of the covenant, God would send them a curse instead. The second half of Deuteronomy 28 is hard to read because God painted a horrifically vivid picture of what would happen if Israel chose to disobey. As we will see, the rest of the Old Testament shows Israel's failure to remain faithful to this covenant and the consequences they suffer for it.

7. *Read Deuteronomy 28. How do these promises of blessing for obedience and cursing for disobedience help us understand the importance of God's covenant with Moses and Israel?*

A Kingdom of Priests

Though God's covenant with Moses promised blessings for Israel, there was more at stake than the well-being of a single nation. Just as God promised to bless Abraham so that he would be a blessing to "all the families of the earth," God intended His covenant with Israel to be a blessing for every nation.

In Exodus 19:5–6, God told Israel that they were to be a "kingdom of priests" and a "holy nation." These two titles are extremely important for understanding Israel's calling. A priest has two responsibilities: to represent a holy God to sinful people, and to represent a sinful people to a holy God. As a kingdom of priests, Israel was meant to represent their God to the nations around them. Collectively, they were to show the world who their God was and what He demanded of the world. On the other side, God meant Israel to represent these nations to Himself. In other words, they were to pray on behalf of the people around them, asking God to bless them. These concepts are also present in the title "holy nation." They were meant to stand out, to be clearly different from other nations. They were set apart for God's purposes. They were to minister on God's behalf, to show the holy character of God to the world around them and be a light to the nations.

As the rest of the Old Testament unfolds, we find that Israel was largely unfaithful to this command. But that did not change God's heart. Israel was still God's "treasured possession," but that did not mean that God wanted Israel to feel superior to the world around them. They were special because God chose them for a specific purpose: to show the world that the LORD is God and to call them into a relationship with Him. God's heart has always been to restore every part of His creation, and He still calls His people to join Him in this work.

8. As a "kingdom of priests" and a "holy nation," what was Israel's responsibility to the nations around them?

9. We are not the nation of Israel, but God uses similar phrases to describe the church (see 1 Peter 2:5, 9). How should God's covenant with Moses and the Israelites affect the way we view ourselves as the people of God?

10. *Spend some time in prayer. Thank God for reaching down into this broken world and choosing to work in and through broken people to accomplish His purposes. Ask Him to give you a heart that is set on obedience and a passion for reaching out to the world around you.*

 Watch the video for this session at multiplymovement.com.

6: Sacrifice and Atonement

This is the best news in the world: God invites humanity into relationship with Him. However, as God makes covenants with people, it creates a serious tension. After all, isn't it impossible for a holy God to stay connected to sinful people? At this point in the biblical storyline some important questions develop. Will God need to lower His standards? (Could He lower His standards even if He wanted to?) Will God's people be able to live sinless lives so they can enjoy God's presence?

Of course, the answer to these questions is no. God would never and could never lower His standards or diminish His holiness. And since the fall, human beings are incapable of living sinless lives and enjoying God's presence on the basis of their own moral purity. So if God is going to bind Himself to human beings, something has to be done about the sin that inevitably enters the lives of the people of God.

God's solution for the problem of sin is sacrifice.

Most Christians today understand that when Jesus died, He was serving as a sacrifice on our behalf. What many don't understand, however, is the major role that sacrifice played in the Old Testament. Most Christians today understand that Jesus's death on the cross paid for our sins and allowed us to have a relationship with God. But we rarely consider that Jesus's death was the culmination of a larger story of sin and sacrifice that develops throughout the Old Testament. Only when we understand the Old Testament sacrifices can we see how the Old and New Testaments dovetail perfectly into one amazing story. Jesus didn't decide on a whim that the problem of sin could be solved by dying on a cross; the Old Testament sacrificial system demanded a sacrifice for sin, and Jesus offered Himself as the ultimate sacrifice on our behalf.

1. *Explain what you already know about the Old Testament sacrifices. Have you ever thought of Jesus's sacrifice in light of the Old Testament sacrificial system? How so?*

Sacrifice in the Unfolding Old Testament Story

Sacrifice is seen throughout the Old Testament. Think back to your study of Adam and Eve. As soon as they ate the fruit that God had forbidden, they felt ashamed of their nakedness and tried to cover themselves with leaves. God's response to this problem foreshadowed the way He would continue to deal with human sin: God made clothes for Adam and Eve out of animal skins. The text doesn't tell us much about the significance of these new garments, but think about it—where did those animal skins come from? Being careful not to read too much into it, we can make a simple observation: an animal had to die so that the shame of sin could be covered. As soon as sin entered the world, God made a way to deal with that sin through sacrifice.

The sacrificial method isn't fully developed or explained until we get to the book of Leviticus, but the unfolding story of the Old Testament does point to sacrifices being made prior to this point. One example from Abraham's life is particularly helpful in understanding how sacrifice works.

In Genesis 22, God asked Abraham to sacrifice his only son, Isaac. At first glance, this request can appear cruel or even absurd. How could God ask Abraham to do such a thing? But as the story continues (and especially the larger story of the whole Bible) the beauty of this request becomes obvious. Keep in mind that God had promised to make Abraham's descendants into a great nation, and Isaac was Abraham's only descendant. Imagine the struggle that Abraham must have gone through. Should he obey the Lord? Wouldn't it make more sense to protect his son in order to pursue the promise that God made to him? Abraham decided to obey the Lord, trusting that God could do anything, including raise his son from the dead (Heb. 11:19). Abraham arrived at the place that God designated for the sacrifice, prepared the altar, and raised his hand to sacrifice his only son. But at the last moment, God stopped him and instead provided a ram for Abraham to sacrifice in place of Isaac.

As amazing as this story is in itself, don't miss what it teaches us about the nature of sacrifice. First, it suggests that God could *potentially* accept a human sacrifice for sin—though He did not allow it to go to this point until the death of Jesus. And second, it shows us that God could accept a substitute—in this case, the ram was sacrificed so that Isaac wouldn't be. Of course, it's not until we see the sacrifice of Jesus in the New Testament that the significance of Abraham's offering becomes clear. Like many things in the Old Testament, Jesus's life, death, and resurrection takes these beliefs and rituals and displays them more beautifully and powerfully than anyone could have imagined.

2.   *Why was sacrifice an important theme in the Old Testament?*

Sacrifice in the Law of Moses

We see occasional sacrifices throughout the first part of the Old Testament, but it wasn't until God gave the Law to Moses that animal sacrifices became an integral part of the life of Israel. The Law encompassed many things. It dictated their civil life and government, their moral behavior, and their religious and ceremonial practices. The Law was specific about when to sacrifice, what to sacrifice, and how to sacrifice. There were a variety of sacrifices or burnt offerings, and each type of offering served a different function. But in general, these sacrifices were designed to show gratitude to God, to demonstrate a contrite heart before God, and to atone for sin.

That word *atone*, or *atonement*, is significant theologically. An easy way to remember the meaning of *atonement* is to break it down like this: at-one-ment. Essentially, atonement is all about reconciling, making amends for what has gone wrong, and reestablishing peace where there was conflict. Atonement allowed people who were distanced from God because of their sin to once again enjoy being "at one" with God. So in addition to providing avenues for expressing love and gratitude for God, the Law of Moses gave the Israelites specific instructions for making atonement for sin. Animal sacrifices gave the Israelites a tangible way of showing their sorrow and desire to have their relationship with God restored. Sacrifices also provided a substitute that could be offered in Israel's place.

A proper understanding of sacrifice and atonement is so helpful for those of us who tend to do good works in hopes of making up for the wrong we've done. Just as the Israelites found atonement through the sacrifices, we must learn to put all of our hope in a sacrifice. The New Testament clearly explains that the sacrifice we must trust in was made by Jesus.

3. *Summarize the role that sacrifices played in the way Israel related to their God.*

A Graphic Reminder of Sin

One of the most striking features of the Old Testament Law is the blood. There seems to be blood splattered everywhere in Leviticus! It's because blood was necessary for an effective sacrifice: "The life of the flesh is in the blood, and I have given it for you on the altar to make atonement for your souls, for it is the blood that makes atonement by the life" (Lev. 17:11).

Try to imagine yourself in ancient Israel. Like every other group of people on the face of the earth, your community is prone to sin. But on a regular basis, you are required to bring the appropriate sacrifices in order to make atonement for your sin and restore peace with God. Every time a sacrifice was offered (which was often), an animal would die, its blood would flow, and the blood would be splattered on the altar. Imagine standing there watching this. It would have been messy, bloody, and smelly. Every time you witnessed this, you would be reminded of the seriousness of sin and its awful consequences. You would see a graphic representation of what your sin requires, and you would be thankful that that lamb, goat, or bull died in your place.

Even though we don't need to make animal sacrifices for sin today, this Old Testament practice still gives us a vivid picture of the seriousness of sin.

4. *How should the Old Testament sacrificial system put our sin into the proper perspective?*

The Day of Atonement

We have already raised the question, "How can sinful humans live in proximity to a holy God?" The answer is found in the sacrificial system generally, but there is one event in the middle of Leviticus that cuts to the heart of this question: *Yom Kippur*, the Day of Atonement (an event that Jews still celebrate today). Every year the Israelites would celebrate the Day of Atonement and God would atone for His people's sins and enable them to dwell with Him.

5. *Read Leviticus 16. What stands out to you from reading this description of the Day of Atonement?*

As we read through Leviticus 16, it is clear that God takes His worship very seriously. The chapter begins as God gave Aaron (Moses's brother and the first high priest) very specific instructions on how to enter His presence. The rest of the chapter describes what is supposed to happen on the Day of Atonement. On this one day out of the entire year, one man out of all the Israelites (the high priest) was allowed to enter the Most Holy Place, the Holy of Holies, and stand before God on behalf of the people.

The high priest was to take with him the blood of a spotless animal. Actually, three animals were involved in this ceremony. First, he was to sacrifice a bull as an offering to atone for his own sins, because he could not come into the presence of God on his own accord—no one, not even the high priest, is holy or perfect. Then the high priest would offer two goats. The first goat would be sacrificed, and its blood would be smeared on the cover of the ark of the covenant just as the bull's blood had been. Picture the significance of this. Inside the Holy of Holies, God's presence was looking down on the ark of the covenant, which contained a copy of the Law that Israel had broken through their sin. Then the lid (also referred to as the "mercy seat") of this ark is smeared with sacrificial blood. This blood satisfied the wrath of God because a substitute was offered in place of the people who deserved His wrath. So instead of seeing the Law that was broken, God looked down and saw the blood of atonement. Essentially, this sacrifice died in place of the entire community of God's people.

Try to picture the intensity of this scene. Imagine waiting outside of the Holy of Holies as the high priest entered to make his offering on behalf of the people. Here was a sinful man entering into the very presence of Almighty God! Imagine the joy you would feel as the high priest safely emerged from God's presence, a sign that the sacrifice had been accepted and your sins had been atoned for.

The priest would then take the second goat (the first goat had been sacrificed), symbolically lay his hands on the head of the goat to represent the sins of the people being transferred to this animal, and then release that goat to "bear all their iniquities on itself to a remote area." This was another powerful picture of what was happening with the sins of God's people. Their sin was being removed, carried off to a remote location, never to visit them again. Their guilt and condemnation were gone.

Keep in mind that as amazing as this feeling of joy over the cleansing of their sin must have been, it inevitably faded. This ceremony was to be repeated every year because Israel would not stop sinning. And the Day of Atonement was supplemented by an ongoing and detailed sacrificial system because Israel's sin was constant. Sin is not an external problem; it runs through the core of each of us and continually manifests itself in a variety of ways. Dealing with sin was therefore an important and familiar part of the everyday lives of the Israelites.

6. *What does the Day of Atonement teach us about the nature of sin and the reality of forgiveness?*

The Problem with Animal Sacrifices

The need to constantly repeat these sacrifices points to a limitation inherent in the Old Testament sacrificial system. But that wasn't the only problem. The effectiveness of these sacrifices was never based on the mere performance of a ritual. From the very beginning, it has been about the heart of the worshipper, not about the value of his or her offering. God said explicitly through the prophet Hosea, "I desire steadfast love and not sacrifice, the knowledge of God rather than burnt offerings" (6:6).

Probably the most startling picture of the shortcomings of animal sacrifice is found in the book of Malachi. In this short book, God spoke forcefully to His people about the uselessness of their sacrifices. They had kept up the outward forms and rituals of the sacrificial system, but their hearts were not behind it. Consequently, they were no longer offering God the best of their flocks; they were simply going through the motions. God said explicitly, "Oh that there were one among you who would shut the doors, that you might not kindle fire on my altar in vain! I have no pleasure in you, says the LORD of hosts, and I will not accept an offering from your hand" (Mal. 1:10).

Surely God would rather have *something* than nothing. Even if what we offer Him is less than our best, He must be pleased that we are giving Him some consideration. Right?

God actually said the exact opposite. He would rather someone shut the doors and prevent sacrifices from being offered at all than to have people making casual sacrifices. Why? Because God is holy and His name is great: "For from the rising of the sun to its setting my name will be great among the nations, and in every place incense will be offered to my name, and a pure offering. For my name will be great among the nations, says the LORD of hosts" (Mal. 1:11). God is actually so offended by these false displays of piety that He threatens to take the dung from their sacrifices and smear it in their faces: "I will rebuke your offspring, and spread dung on your faces, the dung of your offerings, and you shall be taken away with it" (Mal. 2:3). This is a vivid reminder that God takes worship and sacrifice very seriously—and so should we!

7. *How should God's emphasis on the heart of the worshipper affect the way we approach God in our worship and in our everyday lives?*

The Ultimate Sacrifice

Everything we have been saying about the Old Testament sacrificial system finds its culmination in the sacrifice of Jesus Christ. The sacrifices that Israel offered on a regular basis laid the groundwork for the coming of Jesus. When He arrived, the full significance of the sacrificial system finally came into view.

Take a minute to read Hebrews 9:11–10:25. This gives you an opportunity to apply what you just learned from the book of Malachi. Here is a way that you can worship God with excellence: Read this passage with all of your heart. Don't just skim through it, but study it carefully, reverently, as an act of worship.

8. *Read Hebrews 9:11–10:25. In light of what you've studied about the Old Testament sacrificial system and what you read in Hebrews, how does the Old Testament system of sacrifice and atonement help us to better understand the significance of Jesus's death?*

9. *Spend some time in prayer. Ask God to affect your heart with the significance of the sacrifice that Jesus offered on your behalf. Ask God to break your heart over the sin in your life. Ask Him to give you the strength and motivation to identify and uproot*

that sin. Pray that your life would be the "living sacrifice" that Paul described in Romans 12:1. And most of all, thank God for sacrificing Jesus as a substitute for you.

 Watch the video for this session at multiplymovement.com.

7: God's Presence on Earth

Does anything matter more than God's presence with us? Think about it: What could be worse than being separated from Almighty God? The Bible is filled with stories that describe the blessings that come with His presence and the horrors that accompany His rejection. God's presence with people is a central theme of the Scriptures.

God made *covenants* to show that He wanted to be present with humanity. He gave the *Law* to show people how to conduct themselves in His presence. And He established *sacrifices* when sin separated people from His presence. So much of what we see in the Old Testament relates directly to the presence of God.

One of the most fascinating features of the Old Testament Law was a tent, referred to as the tabernacle. This was where God would meet with His people. God had been leading Israel through the desert as a pillar of cloud by day and a pillar of fire by night. With the tabernacle, God was creating a home for Himself on earth. The tabernacle would go with Israel wherever they went—from this point on Israel would be known as the people who literally had God dwelling in their midst.

The establishment of the tabernacle and the presence of God on earth were huge events. But in order to understand the full significance of what was taking place here, we need to go back to the beginning of the story.

God's Presence in the Garden

In the perfect world that God created, humanity lived in the presence of God. In the garden of Eden, Adam and Eve could interact with God without the division that comes through sin. They lived in peace with God, His creation, and one another. The distance we feel from God now was not a part of the human experience prior to the fall. But as we've seen, the fall changed everything.

When Adam and Eve rebelled against God, their fellowship with Him was destroyed. First Adam and Eve broke the relationship by sinning, then they tried to hide from God's presence when He entered the garden. This separation was only intensified when God expelled them from the garden and placed an armed angelic guard at its entrance. Since then, nothing has been more important for humanity than regaining God's presence.

1. *Why is the presence of God so important for humanity?*

The Tabernacle

After Adam and Eve walked out of the garden, people struggled to find the presence of God. Of course, God's presence is literally everywhere, and He was active throughout the Old Testament, just as He is active today. But encounters with God only show up here and there, and God's presence—in the sense that Adam and Eve experienced it—was missing. This is why the tabernacle is so significant. God was offering a solution to what went wrong in the garden. His presence was gone, but now He would live with His people again.

In the previous session, we focused on the Old Testament sacrificial system. This sacrificial system centered on a specific location: the tabernacle. The tabernacle was essentially a tent where God's presence would dwell on earth. The centerpiece of the tabernacle was the ark of the covenant. This ark was basically a box, covered in gold, that contained a copy of the Ten Commandments, a jar of the manna that God used to miraculously feed the Israelites as they journeyed through the wilderness, and Aaron's rod, which God had caused to bud as a sign of His life-giving power. On top of the ark were two cherubim, and God's presence sat atop the ark, enthroned between these angelic figures.

The tabernacle was God's creating a way for His presence to dwell on earth in the midst of His people. Because the laws governing the tabernacle, its design, and the ceremonies involved are so complex, it is easy to miss the significance of the tabernacle as we read the Old Testament. The stunning truth was that God once again blessed His people with the greatest gift He could give: Himself.

At this point in Israel's history, God still led them from place to place with a pillar of cloud or fire. Every time God wanted His people to stop, His presence would descend on the tabernacle until it was time to move on again. The tabernacle meant that God would now be with His people wherever they went. It was a clear sign of God's presence on earth. It was a glimpse of the kingdom of God in the midst of the kingdoms of this world. It was a taste of the garden of Eden that went with them from place to place.

2. *Read Exodus 25:8–9 and 17–22. What is so significant about the tabernacle and the ark of the covenant?*

God's Blessing without God's Presence

Before Israel had a chance to take God's presence for granted, they almost lost it. As soon as God delivered the covenant to Moses on Mount Sinai, Moses walked down the mountain to convey it to the people. But what Moses encountered was shocking. He left a discussion with God Himself only to find the people of Israel dancing and worshipping a golden calf that they had created. The first two commandments (Moses had just watched the finger of God carve these into stone) were "You shall have no other gods before me" and "You shall not make for yourself a carved image … for I the LORD your God am a jealous God" (Ex. 20:3–5). It seemed that God's covenant with Israel was over even before it began.

The way that God responded to Israel's idolatry was devastating in at least two ways. First, about three thousand men died as a direct result of their sin. Second, the nation of Israel came uncomfortably close to losing the presence of God. In Exodus 33, God reaffirmed His promise to give Israel the land He had promised them, but He added a twist. He basically said, "I have promised to give the land of Canaan to you and your descendants. Now go and take it, but I will not go with you. I will send an angel to lead you instead."

The language that God used in Exodus 33 has changed drastically from what we have seen thus far. He referred to Israel as "the people" instead of "my people." Even in sending an angel as a replacement for His presence, God's language was impersonal. He said He would send "an angel," when previously He had talked about "my angel" (compare Ex. 23:23 and 32:34).

Keep in mind that in the preceding chapters, God had outlined the plans for the tabernacle. God had just said, "Let them make me a sanctuary, that I may dwell in their midst" (25:8). Now we see Him using the same terminology to express a devastating concept: I will not dwell among you (33:3).

At this point, Israel was facing life without God. As terrible as that sounds, think about what God was really offering here. God was offering to bless the Israelites apart from a relationship with Him. From a practical standpoint, this makes a lot of sense. The people are going to keep on sinning, so maybe it would be easier if they accepted God's blessing and went on their way.

And sadly, isn't this exactly what most people today really want? God's presence is nice, but what we really want is what He can give us.

3. *Read Exodus 33:1–6. What makes this such a devastating pronouncement for the Israelites?*

4. *Consider God's presence in your own life. How would you respond to the prospect of God's blessing apart from God's presence? Forget about how you "ought" to answer this, try to answer honestly.*

At this moment in history, Israel was standing at a crucial turning point. Moses's response to God's offer of the Promised Land without His presence shows that Moses knew exactly what was at stake here. He said:

> If your presence will not go with me, do not bring
> us up from here. For how shall it be known that I
> have found favor in your sight, I and your people?
> Is it not in your going with us, so that we are dis-
> tinct, I and your people, from every other people
> on the face of the earth? (Ex. 33:15–16).

Moses recognized that Israel had no hope—that there was no point in being the nation of Israel—if they did not have God with them. God's presence is what made them distinct. Israel could not be the people of God without the presence of God.

5. *Read Exodus 33:7–23. What stands out to you about Moses's response?*

6. *As you think of the experiences Moses and Israel had with God, how might it affect the way you interact with God?*

The Temple

Ultimately, God went with His people, and they carried the tabernacle from place to place until God gave them the land of Canaan as He had promised. After Israel was well established in the land, David became the king of Israel. David decided that he wanted to build a temple, a permanent dwelling to replace the tabernacle. Because

David had been a man of war, God told David that his son Solomon would build the temple instead.

It took Solomon seven years to build the temple. It was carefully constructed and elaborate. When it was finally completed, Solomon dedicated the temple to God, and there was a tremendous celebration as God filled the temple. Just as God's presence had resided in the tabernacle, now it would fill the temple. The most significant difference between the tabernacle and the temple was that the temple was not portable. Remember back to Abraham and to God's promise that He would give Abraham and his descendants the land of Canaan. Now that God had fulfilled that promise and His people were living in that Promised Land, God decided to take up a permanent, stationary residence on earth. The land of Canaan, the Promised Land that He had given to Israel, was the one place out of the whole world where God chose to dwell.

With the temple, God was delivering a powerful visual message. Though mankind had rebelled against God's authority, God was reestablishing His reign on earth. The kingdom of Israel, with the elaborate temple in its midst to house the presence of God, was a glimpse of what the world ought to be. It was a picture of God's dwelling in the midst of His earth, ruling over and blessing His people.

When Solomon finished construction on the temple, he dedicated it with a solemn prayer. This prayer shows that Solomon understood the importance of this moment in human history.

7. Read 1 Kings 8:1–13 and 27–30. What does this passage reveal
    about God's glory and the significance of God's dwelling among His
    people?

An Important Warning

As soon as God's glory descended and filled the temple, God
warned Solomon that His presence would dwell among them only
as long as they remained faithful to His covenant and obeyed His
Law. In other words, God was dwelling in the midst of His people,
but only as long as their lives acknowledged His presence. As soon
as they began to take God and His presence for granted, as soon
as they turned their backs on God and His commands, then He
would leave them to their sin. Instead of the blessing that comes
with God's presence, Israel would experience the judgment that
comes with rejecting God.

8. Read 1 Kings 9:1–9. What does God's warning to Solomon teach us
    about what it means for God's presence to dwell in the midst of His
    people?

Tragically, God's warning in 1 Kings 9 became a reality. In the book of Ezekiel, God's people found themselves in exile as a punishment for rejecting God's reign (we will discuss this more in a future session). Ezekiel records the glory of God departing from the temple (Ez. 10–11), an event that was just as dramatic as God's glory filling the temple in 1 Kings 8. Once again, God's people found themselves alienated from God's presence on earth. It had become clear that the tabernacle and temple would not be the ultimate solution, so how would humanity be able to live in God's presence?

God Became Flesh

Once again, Jesus solves the problems raised by the events in the Old Testament. John opened his gospel by describing Jesus as the Word, who was with God in the beginning, and who was God. Then John said something that is shocking in light of what we've been saying about God's presence on earth: "The Word became flesh and dwelt among us, and we have seen his glory, glory as of the only Son from the Father, full of grace and truth" (John 1:14).

That phrase, "The Word became flesh and dwelt among us," carries huge significance. The word John used for "dwelt" literally means "set up a tent." John's word is a Greek translation that comes from the Hebrew word for "tabernacle" used in the Old Testament. So John was announcing that the tabernacle has once again returned, but this time, the tabernacle exists in the person of Jesus Christ. With Jesus, the problem of God's presence among people is solved once and for all. Jesus shows us what it looks like for people to dwell with God and what it means for humanity to embody the presence of God. With Jesus, we never have to worry about losing the presence of God—He came and dwelt among us, and we are joined to Him because of His death on the cross.

Beyond that, God's presence now dwells in us through the Holy Spirit! In fact, Paul said that we are "a temple of the Holy Spirit" (1 Cor. 6:19). He said that we are joined together as the church and we grow "into a holy temple in the Lord" (Eph. 2:21). In Jesus we are "being built together into a dwelling place for God by the Spirit" (v. 22).

9. *How does what you have studied thus far help you understand the significance of God becoming man in Jesus and of the church being identified as a dwelling place for God?*

God's Presence Will Fill the Earth

We will discuss this in greater depth at the end of the New Testament section, but the Bible ends with a beautiful vision of God's glory filling the entire earth (Rev. 21–22). From the moment that the Holy Spirit filled the early church in Acts 2, God's presence has dwelt on earth through His church. But when Jesus returns to set the world to rights, the whole world will be filled with God's presence. What Adam and Eve enjoyed in Eden will be experienced on every point on the globe as renewed humanity enjoys God's renewed presence in a renewed creation.

10. *Spend some time in prayer. Ask God to help you understand the significance of His presence on earth, and to help you live together with the other Christians in your life in a way that reflects His presence and glory in your midst.*

 Watch the video for this session at multiplymovement.com.

8: The Kingdom of God

Finally, after years of Israel's sin and struggling in the desert, God marched His people into the Promised Land! Israel witnessed God's unmatched power firsthand as their army consistently destroyed enemies that were far bigger and much better armed.

At this point in the story, you would think that we would see Israel thriving, rejoicing in God's power, enjoying God's presence, walking in His ways, and living happily ever after. But tragically, that is not how the story goes. Whereas the book of Joshua records God's faithfulness in delivering the Promised Land to Israel, the book of Judges records Israel's unfaithfulness and refusal to live as God intended. Judges feels like a roller coaster: Israel falls into sin and apathy; God raises up a leader to deliver them; the people once again acknowledge God; Israel again falls into sin and apathy; God again raises up a leader to deliver them, and on and on it goes.

But Israel entered a more hopeful period as Samuel came on the scene. Samuel was a prophet of God and the last of the judges.

With Samuel, Israel received a godly leader who faithfully delivered God's word to the people. It was during this time that Israel became a monarchy. But to understand the significance of this shift, we have to look back to the beginning once again.

The King of Creation

Maybe you have never thought about the creation account this way, but Genesis 1 and 2 present God as the King of creation. This King is so powerful and His word is so authoritative that He has only to speak to call things into existence. Genesis 1 and 2 depict the King creating a realm over which He will rule. In the garden of Eden, everything functioned in perfect harmony; everything operated in perfect submission to the King's rule. In the first pages of the Bible we find a beautiful picture of what the world looks like when everyone and everything joyfully embraces the King's reign.

Though we often see human beings rejecting God's authority and trying to establish their own, God originally created humanity to rule on His behalf:

> Then God said, "Let us make man in our image, after our likeness. And let them have dominion over the fish of the sea and over the birds of the heavens and over the livestock and over all the earth and over every creeping thing that creeps on the earth."

> So God created man in his own image,
> in the image of God he created him;
> male and female he created them.

> And God blessed them. And God said to them, "Be
> fruitful and multiply and fill the earth and subdue
> it and have dominion over the fish of the sea and
> over the birds of the heavens and over every living
> thing that moves on the earth." (Gen. 1:26–28)

The picture we are given here is of God, the absolute Ruler over creation, delegating His authority to mankind. We were created to mediate God's gracious rule to every part of His creation. Humanity was made to function under God's kingship.

But when Adam and Eve ate the forbidden fruit, they abused their freedom and rejected God's kingship. With this simple act, God's rule on earth was challenged. Adam and Eve chose to follow the serpent, Satan. This reversal is so significant that Satan is now referred to as "the ruler of this world" (John 12:31). The reality in which we now live would have seemed inconceivable to Adam and Eve before the fall. Could God's kingship really be disputed in the world He created? Would humanity really reject God's reign and live in defiance? As strange as it would have sounded before the fall, this is the struggle we experience every day of our lives.

1. *Take a minute to think about what you learned about God by reading Genesis 1 and 2. How is God's kingship established and displayed in the creation account?*

The True King of Israel

We get another powerful picture of God's kingship when He led His people out of slavery in the exodus. Through the ten plagues, God showed that He was the supreme Ruler of this world—He entered the dominion of Pharaoh and of Egypt's gods and asserted His ultimate authority. By defeating the false gods of Egypt and leading His people victoriously out of slavery, God demonstrated that He was the true King of Israel and of the whole earth.

The covenant that God made with His people at Mount Sinai was an expression of His kingship. This type of covenant, where the conquering king would establish terms for how his people would relate to him, was common for nations at the time. We can see this clearly in Exodus 19:5–6:

> Now therefore, if you will indeed obey my voice
> and keep my covenant, you shall be my treasured
> possession among all peoples, for all the earth is
> mine; and you shall be to me a kingdom of priests
> and a holy nation.

God was the King, and Israel was His kingdom. The tabernacle and the temple were dwelling places for the King—they were His palaces. Remember that the ark of the covenant, where God's presence dwelled, was the centerpiece of the tabernacle and the temple. The Bible actually refers to the ark as the footstool of God's throne (1 Chron. 28:2, Ps. 132:7). This shows us that the tabernacle and temple were about more than containing God's presence as some sort of good-luck charm or spiritual force. These dwelling places acknowledged the kingship of God; they were a reminder that God was in the midst of His people, ruling over and caring for them.

After God led Israel into the Promised Land, the people consistently chose to move away from God and the clear direction He had laid out for them at Sinai. Instead, they chose to do whatever seemed good to them at the time. We read in the book of Judges: "In those days there was no king in Israel. Everyone did what was right in his own eyes" (17:6, 21:25). Not only does this statement indicate that Israel ignored God's laws, it also suggests a solution: Israel needed a king. God was the rightful King of Israel, but they were unwilling to view Him as such. It looked as if God's kingdom would never be fully established in Israel.

Israel Takes a King

At first glance, it might seem like a good idea for Israel to be ruled by a human king. The period of the Judges was chaotic, so it would make sense to establish a clear ruler who would lead and govern the people. Besides that, every nation that surrounded Israel had a king, so they must have felt conspicuous. All they had was a tent and an imperfect series of leaders whom God appointed to govern His people for a time. Wouldn't they be better off with a human king?

This is the line of reasoning that led Israel to ask God for a normal king. Read the account in 1 Samuel 8 and pay special attention to the warnings that God gave about what was really at stake with this decision.

2. *Read 1 Samuel 8. What does this passage tell us about the significance of Israel's choosing to be ruled by a human king?*

The problem is apparent right away: Israel wanted a king so they could be "like every other nation." But Israel had never been like the other nations—and that is basically the point throughout the Old Testament. Israel was to be unique because their God was unique. They were set apart from everyone else because they had Almighty God dwelling in their midst. Becoming like the other nations was a huge step in the wrong direction. God warned them of this, but they didn't see the significance of what they were doing. In choosing a human king, Israel was rejecting God as their king.

First, God appointed Saul as the king of Israel, but he turned out to be a poor representative of God's reign. The people learned firsthand why God had warned them about taking a human king. Once again, Israel had come to a dead end. Israel's history continually teaches us that if it weren't for God's plan and His persistent grace, all hope would have been lost long ago.

God's Covenant with King David

But God still had plans for Israel. When God rejected Saul as king, He called Samuel to anoint David, a shepherd, as the next king. The concept of anointing is important. The king of Israel would literally be anointed with oil, and then he would be known as "the Lord's anointed," an idea that finds its fullest expression in Jesus.

Though it took some time and confidence in God's promise to him, David eventually became the earthly king through whom God would relate to His people as the heavenly King. David was far from perfect, but the Bible describes him as a "man after [God's] own heart" (1 Sam. 13:14), and he set the ideal for what the king of Israel should look like.

The significance of what God would accomplish through David is brought out in 2 Samuel 7, where God makes a covenant with David. In the context of this chapter, David looked at all the blessings the Lord had given to him and decided that he would honor the Lord by building a house for the ark of the covenant. (This "house" would be the temple we looked at in the previous session.) God said that David would not build the temple—this task was left to Solomon, his son—but God also affirmed His purposes for David by making a covenant with him. This covenant built upon the covenants that God made with Abraham and with Moses. It also expanded these covenants and made promises that find their perfect fulfillment in Jesus.

3. Read 2 Samuel 7. What promises did God make to David in this passage?

God's covenant with David shows that He is still at work to fulfill His promises to Abraham. Think back to God's covenant with Abraham. In Genesis 12:1–2, God promised to make Abraham's name great. In Genesis 15:18, God promised to give Abraham and his descendants the land of Canaan. In Genesis 17:3–7, God told Abraham that He would continue His covenant with Abraham's descendants and that from Abraham would come nations and even kings.

Now consider what God promised to David in 2 Samuel 7. God promised to make David's name great (v. 9), to plant Israel in the land of Canaan (v. 10), and to raise up David's offspring and keep David's line on the throne (v. 12). The promises that God made to Abraham were reiterated in the covenant He made with Moses and now again in the promises He made to David. Despite Israel's faithlessness, God was still at work to accomplish His purposes for His people.

Before Israel entered the Promised Land, God prophetically told His people that after they settled into the land they would reject Him and choose to be ruled by a human king (Deut. 17). Knowing this would happen, God had already established a way for Israel to continue to pursue His purposes for them as a kingdom. The intent was that God would reign as King over His people through His relationship—His covenant—with this earthly king. The earthly king of Israel would follow God's rule and submit to God's reign. In doing so, he would be a reflection of the true King of Israel. In addition to this, God continued to give Israel prophets who would hold the power of Israel's kings in check, showing that God is the true King and ensuring that these human kings were ruling on God's behalf.

The Coming King

What God did through David as the king of Israel is a picture that reflects what He had been doing through His people from the time He formed them. But it also points forward to what God would do through His Son, Jesus Christ. It shouldn't surprise us that David ultimately failed to be the perfect king of Israel. He failed in several respects, most memorably by impregnating Bathsheba and then having her husband murdered in an effort to hide his sin. David received God's forgiveness and was still the standard by which all other kings were compared, but his imperfect obedience left God's people longing and waiting for another Ruler.

The prophets continued to revisit the idea that a Ruler was going to come from the line of David and that this Ruler would put the kingdom of Israel—and all the kingdoms of the earth—back in order. This coming King would restore the world to what it was intended to be. Isaiah 11 describes this King as a "shoot from the stump of Jesse" (Jesse was David's father) upon whom the Spirit of the LORD would rest. He would rule Israel and the nations perfectly. Jeremiah 23:5–6 describes the King as a "Branch" from the line of David who will "reign as king and deal wisely" and whose name would be "The LORD is our righteousness." Ezekiel 34:23–24 describes the coming King as a perfect shepherd for God's people. Amos 9:11–12 says that God will rebuild the fallen house of David, and Hosea 3:5 envisions Israel once again pursuing the LORD under the reign of "David their king."

God's future for Israel was very much tied to the concept of Israel as a kingdom under the reign of the Lord's Anointed, who would mediate God's sovereign rule. Notice the imagery God used as He spoke about the future of His people in Ezekiel 37:

My servant David shall be king over them, and they
shall all have one shepherd. They shall walk in my
rules and be careful to obey my statutes. They shall
dwell in the land that I gave to my servant Jacob,
where your fathers lived. They and their children
and their children's children shall dwell there forever, and David my servant shall be their prince
forever. I will make a covenant of peace with them.
It shall be an everlasting covenant with them. And I
will set them in their land and multiply them, and
will set my sanctuary in their midst forevermore.
My dwelling place shall be with them, and I will be
their God, and they shall be my people. Then the
nations will know that I am the LORD who sancti-
fies Israel, when my sanctuary is in their midst
forevermore. (vv. 24–28)

4. *Spend some time thinking about these promises of a coming King
    (consider looking up the passages mentioned in the last two para-
    graphs). How does the concept of a King arising from the line of
    David set the stage for Jesus's arrival in the New Testament?*

Searching for the Kingdom of God

After the reign of King David, Israel had a disappointing line of kings. Eventually, the kingdom of Israel grew so wicked that God sent them away from the Promised Land and into exile (a period in Israel's history that we will explore in the next session). Once Israel lost the kingdom, their national identity was at stake. They desperately wanted to regain the kingdom. But not until the arrival of Jesus would this become a reality.

The books of Ezra and Nehemiah record a partial return of God's people from exile, but there is still no kingdom. The book of Daniel promises that the kingdom will come in the future and that the "Son of Man" will rule all the nations.

As we turn the last pages of the Old Testament and begin reading the New Testament, we find that the kingdom of God is still a major issue. In fact, Jesus came onto the scene preaching "the gospel of God," saying, "The time is fulfilled, and the kingdom of God is at hand; repent and believe in the gospel" (Mark 1:14–15). This is an incredibly exciting proclamation in light of Israel's history as a kingdom! The kingdom has finally come—the good news that Jesus was preaching was that the kingdom of God had once again returned and Jesus was there to rule as God's anointed! In fact, from the moment Jesus's birth was announced, it was clear that He was the coming King, the Ruler from the line of David who would bring the perfect kingdom of God to earth.

5. *Read Jesus's birth announcement in Luke 1:26–33. How does the language used here help us see Jesus in light of the Old Testament kingdom?*

6. *Why is it important for us to see Jesus as the culmination of the kingly line of David?*

When the angel announced Jesus's birth, he used essentially the same terminology that we saw in 2 Samuel 7 when God made His covenant with David. Jesus was the true King of Israel:

> You will conceive in your womb and bear a son, and
> you shall call his name Jesus. He will be great and will
> be called the Son of the Most High. And the Lord
> God will give to him the throne of his father David,
> and he will reign over the house of Jacob forever, and
> of his kingdom there will be no end. (Luke 1:31–33)

We have almost arrived at the New Testament. Most of us are more familiar with the teaching of the New Testament, but understanding the Old Testament helps us see more clearly what the New Testament is telling us. Ultimately, the New Testament is all about Jesus Christ. That term *Christ* is a title, not a last name. It is actually the Greek translation of the Hebrew word for "Messiah," or "Anointed One." When Jesus walked onto the scene, He came as the anointed King of Israel. His role is to mediate the sovereign reign of God over His earth and His people. We still have a part to play in this, but first we need to see that the kingdom of God has a long history.

7. *How should the kingship of God and of His Anointed affect the way we view our relationship to God and His Son?*

8. *Spend some time in prayer. Pray that God would help you to lovingly submit to His rule as the King of creation. Pray that God's reign over this world would be established and that this rebellious world would see Jesus as the true King.*

 Watch the video for this session at multiplymovement.com.

9: Exile and the Promise of Restoration

God's Faithfulness and Israel's Disobedience

Time and again, God was faithful to keep His promises to His people. He multiplied Abraham's descendants into a great nation; He planted the Israelites in the land of Canaan, and He established David's kingly line. But God had also promised Israel that if they disobeyed, they would be conquered by a foreign nation, pulled from their homeland, and led into exile. God had promised this judgment if Israel disobeyed Him, and after generations of patiently waiting for His people to repent, God remained faithful to His promise.

It's hard to read the Old Testament without being blown away by Israel's constant disobedience. As Moses led the Israelites through the wilderness, they continually complained. When Moses went onto Mount Sinai to receive the Law from God, they created a golden idol and worshipped it. When God placed them in the land of Canaan, they kept turning away from Him to worship idols. Idolatry shows up throughout Israel's history. Though there were times of reform, Israel seemed bent on rejecting God. God dealt with this idolatry patiently, but His justice would not be detained forever.

The Curse for Disobedience

When God made His covenant with Moses and Israel, He gave them the Law to show them exactly what was expected of them as the people of God. He promised them that if they obeyed His Law, they would be blessed and would live in the land of Canaan in peace and security. But if they disobeyed, God promised them that they would experience His judgment rather than His blessing. Among other things, this meant that they would be pulled away into exile.

1. *Read Deuteronomy 28. Based on what you have studied in the previous sessions, how did the blessings offered in verses 1–14 become a reality in the life of Israel?*

2. *Summarize the judgments in verses 15–68 that God said would come upon Israel if they disobeyed.*

The Promise of Exile

Every one of the judgments listed in Deuteronomy 28 is terrifying. Israel was defined by their unique relationship with God. They were known for receiving special favor from God, so the thought of experiencing God's judgment rather than His blessing would have been devastating. The promises of agricultural failure and military defeat were bad enough, but the exile brought a much deeper level of judgment. Israel would be abandoned by God, defeated by a distant enemy, and then torn from the land that God had given them. Without the presence of their God and the land He had given them, Israel would lose their identity.

Imagine the horror of hearing these words from God:

> The LORD will bring you and your king whom you set over you to a nation that neither you nor your fathers have known. And there you shall serve other gods of wood and stone.... Because you did not serve the LORD your God with joyfulness and gladness of heart, because of the abundance of all things, therefore you shall serve your enemies whom the LORD will send against you, in hunger and thirst, in nakedness, and lacking everything. And he will put a yoke of iron on your neck until he has destroyed you. (Deut. 28:36, 47–48)

If Israel would not serve their God, they would end up serving their enemies. They would worship carved images, crying out to blocks of wood and stone to deliver them. Notice that when God spoke these words, it was merely a warning: Israel had not even entered the Promised Land by this point. Yet Israel's disobedience was inevitable, and the only real surprise was how long God waited before punishing Israel.

A Divided and Defeated Kingdom

We mentioned in the previous session that the book of Joshua shows Israel's taking over the land of Canaan, and that the book of Judges records the chaos, apathy, and idolatry that characterized Israel after they had settled into the land. We also talked about David's becoming the king of Israel and God's promise to establish His kingly line. But a mere generation after David's kingship, the Israelites became so stubborn and power hungry that they ended up dividing into two camps: the northern kingdom of Israel and the southern kingdom of Judah.

Israel never fully recovered from this split. The northern kingdom (Israel) was almost completely godless—they followed ungodly kings into every form of sin. The southern kingdom (Judah) had a few good kings and experienced some good years, but overall they followed the same pattern of ungodliness and idolatry. In 722 BC, Assyria conquered the northern kingdom of Israel and carried them away into captivity. The southern kingdom of Judah should have learned from Israel's mistakes—God allowed them to hold on for over one hundred years longer, but eventually they suffered the same fate. In 597 BC, Babylon conquered Judah and carried them off into captivity.

3. Read 2 Kings 17:1–23. This passage describes Israel's being taken into exile. The author did not simply describe the event; he included

a theological explanation for what happened. According to this passage, why was Israel sent into exile?

God's judgment on Israel was totally appropriate in light of what they had done, but it is important to recognize that this was never God's intention. In other words, God didn't want to send His people into exile. Hear the anguish in God's voice as He lamented the loss of His people:

> How can I give you up, O Ephraim?
> > How can I hand you over, O Israel?
> How can I make you like Admah?
> > How can I treat you like Zeboiim?
> My heart recoils within me;
> > my compassion grows warm and tender. (Hos. 11:8)

God hated the exile, and the history of Israel shows that He moved slowly and regretfully toward it. God kept sending prophets to warn His people, but they refused to listen. Ultimately, Israel chose exile for themselves, and God remained faithful to His promise to punish Israel for their rebellion.

4. *In light of Israel's persistent rebellion, why do you think it still grieved God to send them into exile?*

Israel in Exile

With the exile, Israel's future seemed uncertain. But God was still working. God still spoke to the exiles through the prophets. Even after removing Israel from their land, God still called them to repent and promised them a future.

How could God still love and pursue His people at this point? They did not love Him, and they proved that through constant rebellion. They had long since turned from God to trust in themselves. They followed foreign kings and worshipped false gods. They deserved the wrath and judgment that God showed them. But they still were not completely destroyed. Why not? The Old Testament is filled with stories of God's destroying entire nations for their godlessness. Why didn't God do this with Israel?

God had too much at stake to destroy Israel. His purposes of redemption were wrapped up in the nation of Israel. They were His people—He had created them, claimed them, and was working out His plan to restore the world through this unique group of people. Israel was known as God's people. When Israel was conquered and taken into exile, the other nations assumed that it was because their God wasn't strong enough to give them military victory. Listen to the way God explained this situation:

> In accordance with their ways and their deeds I judged them. But when they came to the nations, wherever they came, they profaned my holy name, in that people said of them, "These are the people of the LORD, and yet they had to go out of his land." But I had concern for my holy

name, which the house of Israel had profaned among
the nations to which they came. (Ezek. 36:19–21)

In this passage, God made it clear that Israel deserved their punishment. But He also gave the ultimate answer as to why He was not
going to give up on His people: His name. He was going to preserve
them out of concern for His holy name.

5. *Read Ezekiel 36:16–38. Why was God promising to restore Israel?
   Why is this significant?*

6. *Look closely at verses 25–27. God promised to cleanse His people, to
   give them a new heart, and to empower them by His Spirit. What is
   the significance of these promises?*

The New Covenant

While Israel was in exile, God made promises to Israel in Ezekiel 36 and other passages. He guaranteed that He would bring them back to the Promised Land. He would once again be their God, and they would be His people. In many ways, God was reaffirming the covenants He made with Abraham, Moses, and David. Without question, Israel's exile would not last forever. In fact, the books of Ezra and Nehemiah record God's amazing provision in sending Israel back to Jerusalem to rebuild the wall and the temple, both of which had been destroyed. But even still, something was missing. Only a relatively small number of Israelites returned to Jerusalem at this time; the rebuilt temple could not match the grandeur of the temple that Solomon had built; the glory of God did not return to the temple, and the kingdom of God was not restored to Israel. God's people knew there had to be more. And there was.

God made huge promises to Israel in Ezekiel 36:25–27 and restored hope to a desperate nation. Israel had become defiled through their idolatry, but God promised to cleanse them. Israel had a heart of stone that was incapable of loving God, but God promised to remove that heart of stone and give them a living heart made of flesh. Israel had proven that they were incapable of obeying God's commands, but God promised to place His Spirit within them and enable them to follow His commands. These promises show that God's plan for His people would involve a lot more than simply bringing them back from exile. God was going to recreate His people. They were going to be changed from the inside out.

Recall from the previous session that God made a promise to David that his kingly line would continue. Even though the kings who followed David failed to be good stewards of God's kingly authority, the prophets believed and taught that a king would come who would establish God's perfect reign over His people. This king would be one of David's descendants, and he was sometimes simply called by the name David. Soon after promising to restore and recreate His people, God told Ezekiel that this coming king would establish a new, eternal covenant with His people:

> My servant David shall be king over them, and they
> shall all have one shepherd. They shall walk in my
> rules and be careful to obey my statutes. They shall
> dwell in the land that I gave to my servant Jacob,
> where your fathers lived. They and their children
> and their children's children shall dwell there for-
> ever, and David my servant shall be their prince
> forever. I will make a covenant of peace with them.
> It shall be an everlasting covenant with them. And I
> will set them in their land and multiply them, and
> will set my sanctuary in their midst forevermore.
> My dwelling place shall be with them, and I will be
> their God, and they shall be my people. Then the
> nations will know that I am the LORD who sancti-
> fies Israel, when my sanctuary is in their midst
> forevermore. (Ezek. 37:24–28)

The promise of a new covenant raises an obvious question. What was wrong with the old covenant? The answer is simple: sin. Because of their sinful hearts, the people of Israel were constantly breaking

God's covenants with them. Throughout most of its history Israel was idolatrous and immoral. The sad reality is that they were incapable of anything different. Despite the hundreds of times that God's prophets called the people to repentance, they continued in their rebellion. But that was all going to change.

Listen to the way Jeremiah described this new covenant:

> Behold, the days are coming, declares the LORD, when I will make a new covenant with the house of Israel and the house of Judah, not like the covenant that I made with their fathers on the day when I took them by the hand to bring them out of the land of Egypt, my covenant that they broke, though I was their husband, declares the LORD. For this is the covenant that I will make with the house of Israel after those days, declares the LORD: I will put my law within them, and I will write it on their hearts. And I will be their God, and they shall be my people. And no longer shall each one teach his neighbor and each his brother, saying, "Know the LORD," for they shall all know me, from the least of them to the greatest, declares the LORD. For I will forgive their iniquity, and I will remember their sin no more. (Jer. 31:31–34)

The new covenant was different in significant ways. In the old covenant, the law was written on stone. In the new covenant, the law would be written on human hearts. Under this new covenant, God's people would no longer get caught up in external religion; they would experience spiritual change—they would be made spiritually alive. Obedience would no longer be a condition for entering the covenant; obedience would be a promise that God's people would experience through the new covenant.

Under the old covenant, God's people came into contact with Him through the mediation of flawed men (the priests). These flawed men would offer up continual sacrifices, and God would patiently pass over their sin. But under the new covenant, God's people would encounter God directly through the mediation of a flawless man—Jesus Christ. And this flawless man offered Himself as a sacrifice once and for all. Jesus's sacrifice did not pass over sin; it paid for sin and permanently removed it.

7. *Take some time to meditate on Ezekiel 36:25–27 and Jeremiah 31:31–34. What makes this new covenant so unique and important?*

It is easy to read the Old Testament and get fed up with Israel. We get tired of their rebellion and want to scream, "Why don't you understand this? Stop worshipping idols! Turn to God!" And to a certain extent, the Old Testament is meant to show us how unwise and destructive our sin can be. But we need to be careful not to be too harsh with the Israelites. In reality, their problem is our problem.

We need to be careful not to get so caught up in their stubborn rebellion that we overlook our own. In fact, Jeremiah described Israel's sin in universal terms:

> The heart is deceitful above all things,
>   and desperately sick;
>   who can understand it? (17:9)

We all face the same problem. Sin is not some external factor that we encounter from time to time. It pervades every human heart. Israel's sin is our sin—we were all covenant breakers by nature and incapable of obedience. And because we faced the same problem that Israel did, the new covenant is good news for us as well. We can now enjoy the benefits of being recreated by God, changed from the inside out.

This new covenant would include the key elements of the older covenants that God had made with Abraham, Moses, and David. It still centered on God and His people—notice that important phrase, "I will be their God, and they shall be my people"—and it still promised restoration for Israel, but the new covenant also included hope and healing for all the nations of the earth (Isaiah 42:6, 49:6, 55:3–5, 56:4-8, 66:18–24). God's plan of redemption had always been to redeem all of His creation, but Israel had lost sight of this calling. The new covenant would bring together Jew and Gentile. When Adam and Eve rebelled against God, the whole world fell under the destructive power of sin. But now with the new covenant, all creation would experience God's power to redeem and restore.

The New Covenant in Jesus's Blood

As the Old Testament draws to a close, we see Israel's future was still uncertain. But we are left with two very important promises: (1) God was going to send His Messiah, a King from the line of David, and (2) God was going to make a new covenant with His people that would recreate them and enable them to follow His rule.

From the moment of His birth, Jesus demonstrated that He was God's Messiah. His ministry demonstrated that He was Israel's true King. And before Jesus was crucified, He gathered His disciples together and celebrated the Passover. Remember that the Passover celebrated God's act of redemption in setting His people free from slavery and that immediately after this exodus, God had established His covenant with Moses and Israel. When Jesus celebrated the Passover with His disciples, He broke the bread and passed around the wine and told His disciples that these elements would now represent His crucified body and His shed blood. With great significance, Jesus took the wine and said, "This cup that is poured out for you is the new covenant in my blood" (Luke 22:20). With Jesus, the new covenant had arrived. And we will continue to discuss the beauty of this as we study the New Testament.

8. *As the Old Testament comes to a close, we see that God promised to send a King in the line of David and to make a new covenant with His people. How should these promises affect our lives today?*

9. *Spend some time in prayer. Ask God to address the sin in your heart and to give you a heart that loves Him and submits to His rule. Thank Him for His promises of redemption and for the amazing reality of the new covenant established in the blood of Jesus.*

 Watch the video for this session at multiplymovement.com.

Part V: Understanding the New Testament

1: Jesus the Messiah

Between the Testaments

From the moment that Adam and Eve sinned, God has been working a plan of redemption. Even through Israel's failures, God's plan remained intact. In our last session on the Old Testament, we noted that God gave Israel two important promises: (1) God would send His Messiah, who would be a King from the line of David, and (2) God would establish a new covenant to restore His relationship with His people.

God's plan could not fail, but the Israelites must have had their doubts. At the close of the Old Testament, most of the Israelites were still in exile. They were separated from the things that gave them their identity. They had been removed from the Promised Land and pulled away from the temple, which was subsequently destroyed. These were major problems for Israel. How could they be the people of God if they could not worship in the temple and offer sacrifices to atone for their sin?

Eventually, many Israelites made their way back to the Promised Land, but it was not the same. The Roman Empire now ruled the land. The Israelites did have some freedoms. Most significantly, Herod built a new temple and allowed them to worship and offer sacrifices there. Nonetheless, they were subject to Roman rule, and Israel looked nothing like a kingdom.

Many Jews still believed that God would restore the kingdom, but they were deeply divided on how they thought this would happen. Various groups of Jews formed based on the way in which they expected the kingdom to be restored. The Pharisees believed that radical obedience to the Law would cause the Messiah to come and remove the Gentiles from power. The Sadducees forged an alliance with the Romans so they could gain status and control the temple. The Zealots hoped for a revolutionary Messiah who would come as a warrior and defeat the pagans. The Essenes believed that the situation in Jerusalem had become so corrupted by both Romans and faithless Israelites that they retreated into the desert so they could please God in isolation. Overall, the situation was confusing and at times seemed hopeless.

It was into this mess of conflicting hopes and ideologies that Jesus was born in the little town of Bethlehem to humble Jewish parents, both from the little town of Nazareth and descended from the line of David.

The connection between the two Testaments is clear. The last two verses of the Old Testament read:

> Behold, I will send you Elijah the prophet before
> the great and awesome day of the LORD comes. And

he will turn the hearts of fathers to their children
and the hearts of children to their fathers, lest I come
and strike the land with a decree of utter destruction.
(Mal. 4:5–6)

Then the New Testament narrative picks up with an old, God-fearing priest named Zechariah. He was in the temple burning incense when an angel appeared and told him that his wife was going to bear him a son who would

> turn many of the children of Israel to the Lord their
> God, and he will go before him in the spirit and
> power of Elijah, to turn the hearts of the fathers
> to the children, and the disobedient to the wisdom
> of the just, to make ready for the Lord a people
> prepared. (Luke 1.16–17)

Getting to the Point

This prophet who came "in the spirit and power of Elijah" was John the Baptist. His role was to point the way to Jesus. And in effect, this is what the entire New Testament does. It presents Jesus's life, teaching, ministry, death, and resurrection in such a way that we must come to terms with Him. From the moment Jesus came on the scene, it was clear that He was different. His actions, teaching, and ministry came as a surprise to virtually everyone who crossed His path. But before we go too far into the story, take a minute to experience the beginning of Jesus's ministry.

1. *Read Mark 1 slowly and thoughtfully. As you read, consider what it must have been like to have seen Jesus say and do these things. What stands out to you from reading this description of Jesus?*

Jesus the Messiah

Jesus once asked His disciples, "Who do you say that I am?" Peter answered, "You are the Christ, the Son of the living God" (Matt. 16:15–16). We are so used to the term *Christ* that it probably doesn't stand out to you. Yet it was significant to Peter, and it should be significant to us as well.

Remember that Israel was waiting for the Messiah, the King who would come from the line of David. When Jesus was referred to as "the Christ," He was being identified as that Messiah. "Christ" is simply the Greek translation of the Hebrew word *Messiah*. So to refer to Jesus as the Christ is huge because we are saying that He is the promised Messiah—the person through whom God would accomplish His plan of redemption. God's ultimate solution to the problem of sin had arrived. Paul even referred to this moment as "the fullness of time," the culmination of human history (Gal. 4:4)! So important is the New Testament claim that Jesus is the Messiah that John wrote his gospel to prove this one point: "These are written *so that you may believe that Jesus is the Christ*, the Son of God, and that by believing you may have life in his name" (John 20:31).

2. *What are some of the answers people in our culture give to Jesus's
   question "Who do you say that I am?" Why are these answers
   inadequate?*

A Man, but More Than a Man

When Jesus began traveling the land of Israel, He created quite a stir.
Imagine how interested you would be if you heard about a man going
around restoring sight to the blind, healing the sick, and even raising
the dead! Think about this for a minute. People who had spent their
entire lives in complete darkness had an encounter with Jesus, and
suddenly they could see. People who were irreversibly maimed or
diseased suddenly became whole again. People who were mourning
the death of a family member sobbed in disbelief as they held their
son or daughter in their arms again. He was doing the impossible! It's
no surprise that Jesus attracted crowds wherever He went.

But before we focus on the supernatural elements in Jesus's life, it
is important to acknowledge one obvious point: Jesus was a real man.
The New Testament shows that Jesus was fully human. Matthew and
Luke do this by recording Jesus's genealogy—Matthew traces Jesus's
family tree back to David and Abraham, while Luke traces it all
the way back to the first man, Adam. We also know Jesus was truly
human because He got hungry (Matt. 4:2), grew tired (John 4:6),
and wept (John 11:35). The most graphic picture of Jesus's humanity

was His excruciatingly painful death on the cross. His agony was real, and He truly suffered. A crown of thorns drew real blood as it was shoved onto His scalp. The whippings He endured and the nails driven into His hands were as painful for Him as they would be for you. Jesus was just as human as you are.

Having said that, however, the New Testament is equally clear that Jesus Christ was *more* than a mere man. In fact, this is one of the teachings that separate Christianity from the religions of the world. The New Testament writers emphasize that Jesus of Nazareth was fully God. While Matthew and Luke recount Jesus's earthly genealogy, John's gospel explains that Jesus did not begin His existence at His human birth. He was eternal. He has always existed. John tells us that He existed with God in the beginning (before creation) and that He was God (John 1:1–3). This means that Jesus was integrally involved in the process of creation (John 1:3), and that before He came to earth, He lived in a perfect relationship with God the Father.[1]

The other gospels also testify that Jesus was divine. Both Matthew and Luke tell us that Jesus was conceived not by a human father but by the Holy Spirit. Matthew tells us that Jesus calmed a storm (Matt. 8:26), while Mark records that Jesus forgave sins (Mark 2:5). In Luke we read of Jesus's knowledge of future events, including the end of history (Luke 21). We could go on and on with such examples, but the point is clear: Jesus is God in the flesh (John 1:14).

---

1   There has only ever been one God, yet the Bible teaches that He
      exists as Father, Son, and Holy Spirit. The concept of the Trinity is a
      profound mystery, but it is essential to the way the Bible describes God.

Jesus Christ was much more than just a great teacher or a prophet of God. He was the only person ever to live in sinless obedience to the Father. He was the unique Son of God, both fully human and fully divine. These truths mean, among other things, that we cannot treat Jesus lightly. Nothing matters more than the way we respond to Jesus.

3. *Why is it important to understand that Jesus was fully human? How should this reality shape the way you think and speak about Him?*

4. *Why is it important to understand that Jesus was more than a man—that He was, in fact, divine? How should this reality shape the way you think and speak about Him?*

The Fulfillment of God's Plan

Many people heard the teachings of Jesus, saw the unexplainable miracles, and understood that He was sent from God. However, many of Israel's so-called religious experts opposed Him. The religious groups in Israel (the Sadducees, Pharisees, scribes, etc.) emphatically rejected Jesus as the Messiah. Much of this was because as Jesus's popularity rose, theirs declined.

The Jewish leaders who rejected Jesus did not have spiritual eyes to see Jesus for who He really was. But before we get overly critical of the first-century religious leaders, remember that our own sin and ignorance often keep us from recognizing Jesus for who He is. As you continue studying, pray that Jesus would open your mind so that you can see Him for who He truly is.

Jesus was clear in identifying Himself as the One who would fulfill God's Old Testament promises. In Luke 24:44, Jesus said, "Everything written *about me* in the Law of Moses and the Prophets and the Psalms must be fulfilled." Did you catch that? The Law of Moses and the Prophets and the Psalms (these three categories combined were a common way of referring to the entire Old Testament) all speak about Jesus. Jesus was saying that when the Old Testament writers wrote about God's plan of redemption and the hope that God was promising to His people, *they were actually writing about Him!*

The Old Testament is filled with references to Jesus, though many of them are subtle. When Adam and Eve sinned, God told Eve that Satan ("the serpent") would bruise the heel of her descendant, but that this descendant would crush Satan's head. This promise from the first pages of the Bible finds its fulfillment in Jesus, who triumphed over Satan on the cross (Col. 2:15; see also Rom. 16:20). When God made His promise to Abraham, telling him that all the nations would be blessed through Abraham and his descendants,

He was referring to Jesus and what He would accomplish (Gal. 3:8). When God made His covenant with Moses and Israel and gave them the Law, everything about that Law would ultimately be fulfilled in Jesus (Matt. 5:17). When God gave Israel the tabernacle and the temple as an earthly dwelling place for His presence, He was providing a picture of God's dwelling with people that would become a literal reality in the person of Jesus (John 1:14). When God promised David that his throne would be established forever, He was ultimately pointing ahead to the coming of Jesus (Phil. 2:9–11, Rev. 17:14).

As you read through the New Testament, it's good to pay attention to all of the times that the New Testament writers cite Old Testament prophecies as a way of explaining the fullness of what was happening in the birth, ministry, death, and resurrection of Jesus.

5. *Why is it important to recognize that Jesus was fulfilling the promises and prophecies made in the Old Testament?*

The Kingdom of God

There is one central message that both John the Baptist and Jesus preached: The kingdom of God had arrived.

In the Old Testament, there was an expectation that God would establish His kingdom in the future. This purpose included salvation and blessing for His people and the defeat of Israel's enemies. This expectation must have added weight to Jesus's announcement at the outset of His ministry: "The time is fulfilled and the kingdom of God is at hand; repent and believe in the gospel" (Mark 1:15).

Many Jews expected God's kingdom to be established at some point, and Jesus claimed that the time was now. The Spirit's power in Jesus's life proved that God's rule was present. The authority of God's kingdom was clearly seen when Jesus cast out demons, healed the sick, ruled over nature, and even raised the dead (John 11:1–46)! Jesus's teaching was also unprecedented, and those who heard it were often astonished at His wisdom. Understanding this kingdom context should prevent us from seeing Jesus's life and teaching as merely a good source for moral instruction. He didn't come just to establish a vague sense of peace in the world, but to reestablish the rule of God over His creation.

While God's kingdom was certainly present in the ministry of Jesus, Jesus also spoke of a fuller expression of the kingdom in the future. In the Lord's Prayer (Matthew 6:9–13) Jesus taught us to pray for God's kingdom to come and for His will to be done on earth. One day, at a time known only to God, Jesus Christ will return to save His people and bring judgment on those who have rejected Him. This is a painful reality as we think of those who have not yet submitted to Jesus. But the kingdom of God is open to all who will enter, and Jesus sends us out as His ambassadors to call the lost to be reconciled to God (2 Cor. 5:20). And for followers of Christ, God's coming kingdom is everything we have been waiting for! The powers over which Jesus ruled during His ministry in the Gospels—Satan, sickness, death, and the curse that haunts creation—will finally be overcome forever. Believers will enjoy their salvation in its fullness with Christ their King.

6. *Based on what you studied in the session on the kingdom of God in the Old Testament, why is Jesus's proclamation of the kingdom of God important?*

7. *How should the concept of the kingdom of God and the reality of Jesus as the King affect your daily life now?*

Life through Death

Jesus is significant on so many levels. As we read through the Gospels, we are amazed at Jesus's power, His compassion, His wisdom, etc. But ultimately, it was very difficult for the Jews to believe that this man was their promised Messiah for one very important reason: He was executed as a criminal.

Israel's history was filled with kings and judges who conquered their enemies, and the prophecies about the Messiah pointed to a victorious king. So it must have been confusing when Jesus began to speak about His death. And they didn't know what to do about this would-be Messiah once He died.

In Mark 8:31–33, Jesus told His disciples that He was going to "suffer many things" and be put to death. (He also foretold His resurrection.) Peter, unable to see how such a course of events could fit with Jesus's mission, replied by rebuking his Master and suggesting another path. A triumphant king who dies on a cross? Who ever heard of that? Yet all of the Gospels describe Jesus's death as central to His mission, and Luke spent almost ten chapters dealing with Jesus's journey to Jerusalem to die (Luke 9:51–19:27).

Before Jesus was born, an angel declared that He would "save his people from their sins" (Matt. 1:21). John the Baptist referred to Jesus as "the Lamb of God who takes away the sin of the world" (John 1:29). The problem of sin had threatened humanity's relationship with God ever since Adam and Eve's disobedience in the garden. In order for God's people to be in a right relationship with Him, sin had to be atoned for. All of the sacrifices that God's people made in the Old Testament pointed forward to the sacrifice that Jesus would offer on the cross (Heb. 9–10). Jesus was the true Passover Lamb (1 Cor. 5:7)—He sacrificed Himself so that we can live.

In the last Old Testament session, we talked about the promise of a new covenant, and the reality that the death of Jesus established this covenant. As we discuss Jesus's death here, we cannot forget this connection with the new covenant. As Jesus celebrated the Passover with His disciples, He held the cup and said, "This cup that is poured out for you is the new covenant in my blood" (Luke 22:20). Thus Jesus fulfilled both of the major promises that carry over from the Old Testament: (1) He was the coming King from the line of David (the Messiah), and (2) through His death He established the new covenant that would heal and recreate His people.

Of course, the ultimate proof of the power of the cross is the resurrection. Many had claimed to be the Messiah, but only Jesus rose from the dead to prove it. After all, a conquering King cannot remain buried in a tomb. The resurrection is crucial to our faith and to the fulfillment of God's saving purposes. Without it, we have no hope. The Gospels testify that Jesus rose from the grave and appeared to His disciples.

8. *Carefully read Ephesians 2:1–10 and Colossians 2:13–15. If you are familiar with these passages, force yourself to read them slowly, as though you've never read them before. What do these passages say about the significance of Jesus's death and resurrection?*

9. *According to these passages, how should we relate to Jesus?*

"Follow Me"

It is critical that you understand the story of Jesus, but understanding the story is not enough. It is not enough to merely absorb the information—you must respond to it. The message of Jesus's death and resurrection demands something of us. Jesus continues to call people—He calls you and me—to follow Him and live, even if it costs us everything. Christ's death and resurrection should give us confidence in the salvation He offers. Listen carefully to the message proclaimed by Jesus's earliest followers:

> What God foretold by the mouth of all the prophets, that his Christ would suffer, he thus fulfilled. Repent therefore, and turn again, that your sins may be blotted out, that times of refreshing may come from the presence of the Lord, and that he may send the Christ appointed for you, Jesus, whom heaven must receive until the time for restoring all the things about which God spoke by the mouth of his holy prophets long ago. (Acts 3:18–21)

10. *Spend some time in prayer. Pray that God would take the truths you have been thinking through and use them to affect your heart. Ask God to help you respond to Jesus appropriately—whether you have never considered Jesus's call to follow Him or you have been walking with Jesus for many years.*

Watch the video for this session at multiplymovement.com.

2: The Great Commission

Jesus's life, death, and resurrection should affect every day of your life. During His short time on earth, Jesus challenged the religious leaders and their assumptions about what it meant to please God. He showed us what God intends humanity to look like, and tore down every barrier that would keep us from being the people God made us to be. Jesus's mission on earth was to see God's power, love, and healing permeate every aspect of this broken world and our broken lives. He came to see God's will done on earth as it is in heaven. One day, Jesus will return to finish this task, to take all things and make them new (Rev. 21:5). But in the meantime, He has given us a mission to accomplish.

The Mission of the Church

In every way, Jesus was what the world had been waiting for. He was the answer for all of Israel's hopes and the embodiment of God's plan of redemption. Nothing could be more important for this world than Jesus's mission on earth. As the disciples began to recognize that Jesus truly was the Christ, the Messiah, they must have seen the importance of what Jesus was doing. Imagine how surprised and disappointed they must have been, then, when Jesus died. And imagine how their excitement must have hit an all-time high when He rose from the grave! This mission to restore the world was back in motion. Jesus could now assume Israel's throne and rule the world in righteousness and peace.

But that's not how the story goes. At least, not immediately. Instead of wrapping up human history then and there, Jesus gave His disciples an all-important task:

> Jesus came and said to them, "All authority in heaven and on earth has been given to me. Go therefore and make disciples of all nations, baptizing them in the name of the Father and of the Son and of the Holy Spirit, teaching them to observe all that I have commanded you. And behold, I am with you always, to the end of the age." (Matt. 28:18–20)

What exactly should the church be doing? The answer has been the same since the day Jesus spoke these words. Sure, each church will have some distinctives, and the church in different places and in different times has had some unique issues that it has needed to address. But the church has one mission. It is the mission that characterized Jesus's ministry on earth, and it is the mission that He left to the church when He returned to His Father.

Our mission on this planet is spelled out here in the "Great Commission." We are called to spread Christ's rule on earth through making disciples. We share the good news of a King who conquered death, and who calls every part of His creation to submit to His benevolent reign. This is what Jesus taught His followers to pray for (Matt. 6:10) and it is the reality He calls us to work toward here on earth.

1. *Read Luke 24 and Acts 1:1–11. As you read, place yourself in the scene and try to feel the significance of these events. How do the circumstances surrounding the Great Commission add significance to Jesus's words?*

The Authority of Jesus

In order to more fully understand what we are called to do here on earth, we will analyze the Great Commission in this session. As Jesus delivered this command to His followers, He began with a very important statement: "All authority in heaven and on earth has been given to me" (Matt 28:18). Here we have the foundation for the Great Commission.

We serve a King who has absolute authority over every square inch of creation. This authority extends not only to animals, plants, and weather patterns, but also to every human being on the planet.

Understanding this truth should give us confidence as we move out into a world that is opposed to God's reign.

Since all authority belongs to Jesus Christ, we are obligated to obey the Great Commission. The command is clear. But this is about more than cold obedience. The King who commands us to make disciples is the same King who sacrificed Himself to give us life. It is our *pleasure* to serve this King, and we should find joy in submitting to His will. Furthermore, it should not be enough that we ourselves enjoy a healed relationship with our King; we should want every person on earth to experience this great salvation.

A Worldwide Mission

Though Jesus entered a specific culture in a specific part of the world, He is more than a local religious figure. Jesus is the Savior given by God for all people, regardless of race, nationality, or any other distinction. And because every person on the planet has rebelled against God (Rom. 3:23), everyone needs the salvation that Jesus offers. Because of this, Jesus calls His church to move out into every corner of the world with this one and only hope of healing and salvation: "And there is salvation in no one else, for there is no other name under heaven given among men by which we must be saved" (Acts 4:12).

Jesus first gave the Great Commission to the early disciples. They took this task seriously, and spread the gospel throughout much of the known world within a relatively short amount of time. Yet the task of taking the gospel to all peoples did not end with them. This worldwide mission belongs to the church, and it ought to characterize our efforts today.

There is no denying that the task of taking the gospel to the nations is massive. There are a lot of people in this world, and a huge percentage of them have no way of even hearing about the gospel. And don't forget about your family members, friends, and coworkers who reject the claims of Christ. Thankfully, we aren't alone in this supernatural task. Making disciples is ultimately God's work, and He will accomplish it in His power. But God's commitment to His plan of redemption does not absolve us from our responsibility to obey His commands. God *will* reach every corner of this world, and He has chosen to accomplish this task by working through His church.

2. *We can get so caught up in our own personal relationships with God that we forget to think about the global implications of the Great Commission. Why is it important to see the mission of the church as a global calling?*

The Call to Make Disciples

With the Great Commission, we are back to where we started in Part I. It all comes down to making disciples. But now we can see that disciple making is rooted in God's plan of redemption. It is central to God's heart for His people, for His world.

As we have said, a disciple is simply a follower of Jesus. If we believe that Jesus is who He says He is and we do what He tells us to do, then we are disciples. So the process of disciple making amounts to telling other people about Jesus and calling them to follow Him as well. Discipleship is a lifelong process where we are continuously made more and more like Jesus.

Jesus said that in making disciples of all nations, we are to baptize them in the name of the Father, the Son, and the Holy Spirit, and to teach them to obey all that He commanded (Matt. 28:19–20). The first step for those who choose to follow Christ and have been transformed by His Spirit, then, is to identify with Christ through being baptized. Just as Jesus was buried in the earth and then raised up into new life, so the new Christian is "buried" under the water in baptism and brought up again as a symbol of the new life he or she has received. Baptism also initiates the new believer into Christ's church where he or she becomes a member of a local body of believers. This initial step is nonnegotiable. It is a command of Jesus Christ, and we should consider it a privilege to identify with Jesus and His people through baptism. Who could put their trust in such an amazingly gracious Savior and not want to identify with Him?

One result of Jesus's command to teach others to obey all that He commanded is the New Testament itself. These gospel accounts and letters were written to believers in various churches in order to tell them more clearly who Jesus was and to deliver ongoing instruction on living as followers of Christ in a hostile world. Salvation is not like receiving a train ticket to heaven, where the ticket gets us aboard, but after that we can put it in our pocket and forget about it. Rather, it is like a marriage, where we enter into a relationship with Jesus Christ and become a part of His family, the church. The Christian life is a process of better understanding what Jesus taught, learning to apply that teaching in our everyday lives, and then teaching others—people directly around us and people on the other side of the globe—to do the same.

3. *Why do you think Jesus would give us the strategy of disciple making as the means for accomplishing our mission on earth?*

4. *Take a minute to consider the significance of baptism. Write down some thoughts below. If you have been baptized, include some reflections on your own experience with baptism.*

5. *What role should teaching play in our Christian lives and in the life of the church?*

The Continuing Presence of Jesus

If the Great Commission sounds impossible to you, that's because it is. As daunting as the task to make disciples of all the nations on the face of the earth would be by itself, we also face serious opposition. Satan, the world, and our sinful desires fight against our growth in the Christian life and the advance of the gospel. Paul warned us that if we are going to live out this mission, we will experience persecution: "Indeed, all who desire to live a godly life in Christ Jesus will be persecuted" (2 Tim. 3:12). This very day, Christians around the world are being persecuted, beaten, and even put to death for identifying with Jesus Christ. We are mistaken if we think our message will always be received warmly.

But while the opposition is real and intimidating, Jesus's final words in the Great Commission should give us courage: "I am with you always, to the end of the age." Jesus's very presence is promised to us so that we do not need to be afraid. Imagine how fearless you would be if you could physically see the Son of God by your side. He promises to be with us. Remember that God's plan has never wavered, and our ultimate victory is assured.

6. *Most likely, you already believe that God's presence is with you as you seek to honor Him in this world. But take some time to meditate on that simple truth: "I am with you always." How should this statement affect your daily life and the way you view your God-given mission?*

The Power of the Holy Spirit

After telling His disciples that they would be His witnesses to the entire world, Jesus's next instruction must have been surprising: "Wait." For many of us, that doesn't sound like great advice. After all, there's a mass of humanity out there that needs the gospel. Don't we need to hit the ground running?

The Great Commission will never be accomplished by human effort or wise planning, though both are crucial for the task. We need God's power in order to carry the gospel into every part of the globe. Only God's power can transform rebels into disciples. This is precisely why Jesus commanded His disciples to wait (Acts 1:4). Before moving out to Judea, Samaria, and the ends of the earth, the disciples had to be empowered by the Holy Spirit for this supernatural task.

7. *Have you ever tried to follow Jesus apart from the power of the Holy Spirit? Why is this approach bound to end in frustration?*

8. *Given your specific setting, what would it look like to pursue the Great Commission through the power of the Spirit?*

Finished and Unfinished

As we consider God's mission here on earth, it is important to recognize what has been finished and what is still unfinished. The New Testament is very clear that the work of salvation is complete. Hebrews says, "When Christ had offered for all time a single sacrifice for sins, he sat down at the right hand of God" (Heb. 10:12). In other words, Jesus did what needed to be done in order to reconcile humanity to God; then He sat down because everything was finished. This means that our message is simple and straightforward: "Believe in the Lord Jesus, and you will be saved" (Acts 16:31).

But we still have a job to do. What remains unfinished is the task of bringing this message to the ends of the earth. God calls us to be His colaborers (1 Cor. 3:9) and ambassadors (2 Cor. 5). We are to carry the good news of what He has done in Jesus Christ to the very ends of the earth and work to see His rule fully established in every corner of the world. This means that we reach out to our next-door neighbors and the masses of East Asia. This is our calling in life. And ultimately, this is where God's plan of redemption has been moving from the very beginning.

If the command to make disciples and minister sacrificially to God's people seems overwhelming, recall Jesus's reassuring words in the Great Commission: "All authority in heaven and on earth has been given to me … and behold, I am with you always, to the end of the age." By the power of the Holy Spirit, the church can fulfill its mission. Actually, Jesus promised that the church *will* fulfill its mission: "I will build my church, and the gates of hell shall not prevail against it" (Matt. 16:18). God chose to fulfill His purposes on earth through His church, and He does not have a backup plan. God will use us as the church to reach the world with the hope and healing found in Jesus Christ.

9. *Read Revelation 7:9–12. This passage gives us a vision of the end of the story. This life will conclude with an enormous community of redeemed people from every nation, tribe, people, and language praising God together for His salvation. How should this vision of the end of the story affect the way we think about our mission now?*

10. *Spend some time in prayer. Ask God to affect your heart with the urgency of the mission He has given you and the other Christians in your life. Ask Him for the strength, wisdom, and perseverance to pursue His mission in the strength of His Spirit.*

 Watch the video for this session at multiplymovement.com.

3: The Spirit of God

Do you feel desperate for the power of the Holy Spirit today? If not, you may have a misunderstanding of who you are or who the Holy Spirit is. Every aspect of our salvation is dependent on Him. Without the Spirit, we can't know God, understand Scripture, overcome sin, or transform the people around us. We are spiritually impotent without the Spirit, so it is vital that we have a right understanding of who He is and what He does.

Our need for God's Spirit goes all the way back to the beginning. Adam and Eve rebelled against God in the garden, and humanity has been rebelling ever since. The history of Israel is a powerful reminder that human beings cannot faithfully follow God without the Spirit. God pinpointed Israel's problem in Ezekiel 36: they had a heart of stone. They were spiritually dead. They needed a new heart and a new spirit. And God's solution to this problem involved nothing less than the complete transformation of His people:

> I will sprinkle clean water on you, and you shall
> be clean from all your uncleannesses, and from all
> your idols I will cleanse you. And I will give you a
> new heart, and a new spirit I will put within you.
> And I will remove the heart of stone from your
> flesh and give you a heart of flesh. And I will put
> my Spirit within you, and cause you to walk in my
> statutes and be careful to obey my rules. (Ezek.
> 36:25–27)

What God's people needed was the Spirit of God. They needed to be changed from the inside out and empowered by the very presence of God. This may have sounded far-fetched to the Israelites. After all, they stood terrified at the base of Mount Sinai when God spoke with Moses on the mountaintop. They fell on their faces as God's glory filled the temple. They had to be so cautious with God's presence dwelling in the tabernacle and temple. How could this all-powerful God possibly dwell within stained and fragile human beings?

Yet this miracle is the exact reality that we find in the New Testament. It is the solution to humanity's rebellion, the culmination of God's plan of redemption.

When Jesus told the disciples of the Spirit's coming, He was not implying that the Spirit had not yet come into existence, or that the Spirit was previously inactive in the world. The Spirit was active in creation and in God's redemptive work in the Old Testament. However, the Old Testament pointed ahead to a time when God's Spirit would work in humanity in a new and powerful way.

1. *Take a minute to consider the significance of the promise of the Holy
    Spirit in Ezekiel 36:25–27. Explain why this promise is so impor-
    tant in the history of redemption.*

Who Is the Holy Spirit?

We must be careful when we discuss a topic as sacred as the Holy
Spirit. The most important thing is to recognize that the Holy Spirit
is God. Just as Jesus Christ is a distinct person but is also fully divine,
so too the Holy Spirit is both unique and fully God.[1] This is the
mystery that we refer to as the Trinity, and it is based in the reality
that the Bible talks about the Father, the Son, and the Holy Spirit
as distinct persons, but also clearly identifies each of these persons
as God.

This carries important implications for how we think about the
Holy Spirit. He is more than a mystical guru or a genie—He is God
and worthy of the love and obedience that God deserves. This also

---

1   One of the most direct statements in Scripture that equates the Holy
    Spirit with God Himself is found in Acts 5. In verse 3, Peter asked
    Ananias why he chose to lie to the Holy Spirit, then in verse 4 Peter
    told Ananias that he had lied to God. The same assumption is made
    throughout the Bible: the Holy Spirit is fully God, just as Jesus Christ
    and the Father are fully God.

tells us that the Holy Spirit is a person. He is not an impersonal force, so we should not refer to the Spirit as an "it." The Holy Spirit is a "He," a person with the ability to act, will, and even be grieved (Eph. 4:30). These brief thoughts should frame the way we think about the Spirit of God.

2. *How should seeing the Holy Spirit as a person and as God Himself change the way you relate to Him?*

The Spirit in the New Testament

The Holy Spirit's actions fill the pages of the New Testament. From the very start we see that John the Baptist and Jesus were filled with the Holy Spirit as they grew and fulfilled their ministries (Luke 1:15 and 4:1). The Gospels are full of reminders that Jesus's ministry was empowered by the Spirit of God. The incredible events that unfold in the New Testament are the direct result of the Holy Spirit's working.

In Acts 2, the Spirit came in dramatic fashion to the disciples and empowered them in an unprecedented way. This came at a crucial moment. Jesus returned from the dead, gave them an impossible task in the Great Commission, and then ascended back to heaven. The disciples had been commissioned, but Jesus told them to wait until they received power from above. Suddenly, the Spirit came upon the disciples, and they began "telling the mighty works of God" in multiple languages. Peter pointed out that this outpouring of the Spirit had been promised in the Old Testament. God's people had been waiting for the Spirit to empower them, and that long-awaited day had arrived. The Spirit of God was now working in humanity—not only on the leaders of Israel but on all of God's people.

3. *Read Acts 2 carefully. As you read, pay attention to two things: (1) references to Old Testament truths and promises and (2) references to the Holy Spirit. What references do you see in Peter's sermon to some of the key concepts you studied in the Old Testament sessions?*

4. *What does this passage say about the Holy Spirit? How was the Holy Spirit working at this significant moment in redemption history?*

The Spirit of God and the Word of God

Not only is the Holy Spirit responsible for the miraculous events recorded in the New Testament, He is also responsible for the writing of the Bible itself! Jesus told His disciples that the Spirit would remind them of what He had been teaching them (John 14:26). These are the things that the disciples and their close associates recorded in the New Testament. Similarly, 2 Peter 1:21 tells us that Scripture is not a human invention, but rather the result of the Spirit's working through the authors of the Bible. Every detail of the text of Scripture, even down to the seemingly mundane grammatical features,[2] is inspired by God and is therefore authoritative. While it is true that God used the personalities and other characteristics of the human authors in recording Scripture, even these human words are referred to as the Spirit's speaking (Heb. 3:7).

The Ministry of the Spirit

When Jesus was ministering on earth, there was no doubt that He was working toward the fulfillment of God's plan of redemption. We might have expected Jesus to continue ministering, gathering more and more followers, and finally completing the redemption that the world was longing for. But just when it seemed that redemption was a possibility, Jesus left. Was God's plan being cut short?

Of course not. Jesus left when He did because that was part of God's plan. Jesus must have stunned the disciples when He said that it would be *better* for Him to leave than to stay! How could that be? How could God's mission on earth possibly proceed more effectively

---

2   For an example of this, see Galatians 3:16, where Paul made an
    important theological argument based on the Old Testament's usage
    of a plural noun rather than a singular.

without Jesus? The answer is found in the Holy Spirit. Jesus said, "I tell you the truth: *it is to your advantage that I go away*, for if I do not go away, the Helper will not come to you. But if I go, I will send him to you" (John 16:7).

Jesus sent us His Spirit ("the Helper") so that we can fulfill God's purposes on earth. The Spirit dwells inside His people—just as God dwelt in the tabernacle and temple in the Old Testament—so that He can work through us. This indwelling of the Spirit is not a special gift for some Christians, but rather it is God's gift to *all* of His people. Paul said very simply, "Anyone who does not have the Spirit of Christ does not belong to him" (Rom. 8:9).

The Spirit is absolutely essential for fulfilling the mission we have been given. Unless the Spirit gives us the power to faithfully follow Jesus, we will follow in the footsteps of disobedient Israel. So great is our need for the Spirit that we are commanded to walk by the Spirit (Gal. 5:16), be filled with the Spirit (Eph. 5:18), pray in the Spirit (Jude v. 20), and put sin to death by the Spirit (Rom. 8:13), among other things. The Spirit secures our faithfulness till the end. Even the assurance that we are God's children comes from the testimony of the Holy Spirit (Rom. 8:16). In Romans 7 and 8, Paul contrasted the life that is lived in the flesh (that is, apart from the Spirit of God) with the life that is lived in the Spirit. The difference is staggering.

5. *Read Romans 7 and 8. What does Paul's comparison of these two ways of living say about the role of the Holy Spirit and our need for Him?*

The Spirit in God's Mission

God's plan of redemption marches on, and He is using His Spirit in the lives of His people to do this work. The church's mission is too difficult to accomplish without relying on the Spirit. Our mission is too important to attempt without His power. We simply cannot fulfill the Great Commission without seeking and depending on the Holy Spirit.

But we do need to be careful that our pursuit of the Spirit leads us toward Jesus, not away from Him. John told us that the aim of the Holy Spirit is to glorify Jesus Christ (John 16:14). Like a spotlight, the Spirit focuses the attention on Christ and His salvation. Therefore, we should not separate the work of the Spirit from the work of Jesus (or God the Father, for that matter). If we are not led to love and trust Jesus Christ more, it's likely that we are out of step with the Spirit.

The Spirit can do unbelievable things in and through us. The miracles recorded in the New Testament often inspire us to pursue similar experiences today. But keep in mind that it is the Spirit we are pursuing, not a specific supernatural experience. As you seek to live by the power of the Spirit, look to the promises of God's Word. Trust the Spirit to show His power however He wants. More often than not, the Holy Spirit guides us by shaping who we are. He gives us new desires so that we gradually begin to live with the goal of glorifying God in all of our decisions. Though this doesn't look as dramatic as healing the sick or foretelling the future, it is every bit as miraculous.

6. *How have you seen the Spirit of God working in the life of your church? If you are having trouble identifying the work of the Spirit,*

why do you think the Spirit's work isn't being clearly seen in your church?

The Spirit of God in the Church

In order to experience everything the Spirit offers, you need to be in close fellowship with other Christians. God designed us to function in a community of believers, each with our own spiritual gifts. To neglect your local church is to cut yourself off from one of the Spirit's most powerful ministries.

All believers need the spiritual gifts of other believers. We need their teaching, leadership, encouragement, mercy, and even their loving confrontation, to name only a few gifts. On the other hand, consider how the Spirit has gifted *you*. How are you supposed to minister to your Christian brothers and sisters?

The Spirit works not simply through individuals, but through the church as a whole. Everyday church life—manifest in things like encouragement, prayer, and communion—may sound very "ordinary," but there's nothing ordinary about God's people. They are a Spirit-filled community; they are God's holy temple. We have already seen that the Spirit dwells within each Christian, just as He dwelled within the Old Testament temple. As important as that truth is, Paul also told us that the church is built *together* into a temple for the Holy Spirit (Eph. 2:19–22). That is, the Spirit does not simply dwell within each one of us, He also dwells in our collective midst. The church is so central to God's mission on earth that He dwells among us to empower us for the work He has called us to.

7. *How are you partnering with other members of the body of Christ to be used by the Spirit in fulfilling God's mission on earth?*

8. *Spend some time in prayer. Thank God for the incredible gift of the Holy Spirit. Pray that you would be empowered to pursue and rely on the Spirit's power in your life. Pray that God would work through the life of your church to bring healing, hope, and change to the world around you.*

 Watch the video for this session at multiplymovement.com.

4: The Early Church

Somewhere along the line, it became popular to pursue Jesus while shunning organized religion. We even hear from people who "love Jesus but hate the church." While no one can deny that the church has its share of problems, Jesus never gave us the option of giving up on His church. And He certainly would not approve of us "hating" her. The church was His idea, so it is impossible to follow Him while shunning the church He died to save.

The reality is that God is using His church around the world to transform lives and accomplish His will on earth. In many ways and in many places the church today is healthy and focused on fulfilling God's mission. But it is also true that much of the church is in a state of disarray. Churches define themselves by virtually every issue under the sun. Christians are known more by their bumper stickers and T-shirts than by the love of Christ. Gossip and hypocrisy run rampant. Many churches are more concerned with preserving the status quo than reaching out to the people around them.

With such a wide array of sentiments about the church, we have to ask some important questions: What is the church? What should the church look like? What should the church be doing? If we can't answer these questions biblically, then we will only be adding to the confusion. If the church doesn't understand its identity and its role in this world, then it is bound to be confused, paralyzed, and ineffective.

When Jesus ascended to the Father, He left one group in His place to carry on His mission: the church. If we don't do everything we can to understand who we are and what we should be doing as the church, then we are not taking Jesus's mission seriously. By God's own choice, the continuation of His plan of redemption now rests on the church.

The Early Church

There is so much that could be said about the church. Peter said that the church is "a chosen race, a royal priesthood, a holy nation, a people for his own possession" (1 Pet. 2:9). Paul called the church a "pillar and buttress of the truth" (1 Tim. 3:15), a temple of the Holy Spirit (Eph. 2:19–22), the body of Christ (1 Cor. 12), and the bride of Christ (Eph. 5:22–33). Each of these descriptions should be explored and discussed at length. But in this session, we will assess the church's identity by examining the founding of the church in Acts 2.

At the beginning of the book of Acts, there were about 120 people who followed Christ. The twelve apostles[1] formed the core of this group. Then came the day of Pentecost. Peter stood up and proclaimed that God had raised Jesus from the dead, the same Jesus whom the crowds had demanded to see crucified. Peter's Spirit-empowered proclamation brought great conviction, and about three thousand people repented of their sins and put their trust in the Lord Jesus Christ. With this unbelievable demonstration of the Spirit's power, the church was born.

There was something so attractive and intriguing about this first group of believers. Not only was the birth of this group miraculous, the way they began to live together and interact was something the world had never seen. Acts 2:42–47 describes life in the early church. Take a minute to think through the way this group is described.

1. *Read Acts 2:42–47 slowly. After you read it, spend a few minutes meditating on what characterized this group of people. What stands out to you?*

---

1   The twelve "apostles" were Jesus's original twelve disciples who followed Him throughout His ministry. After Judas betrayed Jesus, he committed suicide and the other eleven disciples replaced him with Matthias in Acts 1. The word *apostle* means "one who is sent," "delegate," or "messenger."

Several things made the early church blatantly stand out. For one, Luke told us that the early church "devoted themselves to the apostles' teaching" (Acts 2:42). They had a deep commitment to what the apostles taught. The apostles' teaching emphasized everything that happened in Christ and the significance of these events. In other words, the apostles were dedicated to the gospel. Their teaching was the fulfillment of what was prophesied in the Old Testament, and this teaching would later be recorded under the inspiration of the Holy Spirit to form the New Testament. So the New Testament we hold in our hands is "the apostles' teaching"—the same truths that the early church was devoted to. God's Word has always been essential to the life of the church.

2.   *Why do you think the early church devoted themselves to the apostles' teaching? What implications does that have for the church today?*

Luke (the author of Acts) also said that the early church was devoted to fellowship. The word *fellowship* sometimes has strange connotations in the church today. If it sounds cheesy, lighthearted, or old-fashioned to you, then you have the wrong idea about fellowship. The first Christians shared their lives with one another. It wasn't about church picnics, potlucks, or small talking in the "fellowship hall." They were real people meeting real needs and joining together to fulfill a real mission. They weren't meeting together because they kind of felt like they should. They shared their lives because in Christ they had everything in common. They truly loved each other. They cared deeply about God and His mission on earth, so they joined with the other Christians around them and worked together toward the goal.

We are called to do the same. In fact, God tells us that fellowship is even more important for us *now* since His return is coming soon: "Let us consider how to stir up one another to love and good works, not neglecting to meet together, as is the habit of some, but encouraging one another, *and all the more as you see the Day drawing near*" (Heb. 10:24–25). Our fellowship has never mattered more than it does right now.

3. *Why was fellowship so important for the early church? Why is it important for the church today?*

The reference to the "breaking of bread" is either a reference to taking the Lord's Supper (communion) together as a body of believers, or to the sharing of meals together. It probably refers to both. The early Christians often took the Lord's Supper as part of a larger shared meal. Both the Lord's Supper and the early church's practice of eating together served as expressions of their common faith in Jesus Christ.

Paul pointed back to the night when Jesus observed the Passover with His disciples and transformed that ritual into what we know as the Lord's Supper. The bread became a reminder of His broken body and the wine of His shed blood. This celebration is a reminder of the new covenant that Jesus made with His people, the church. Paul highlighted the significance of this ritual: "As often as you eat this bread and drink the cup, you proclaim the Lord's death until he comes" (1 Cor. 11:26). In taking communion, we are proclaiming that Jesus's sacrifice is central to our mission and our life together as the church.

4. *In your own words, describe why the Lord's Supper is significant. Does communion carry this significance in your church? Why or why not?*

Luke also told us that the early church was devoted to prayer. To say that prayer was important to these early Christians would be a gross understatement. Immediately after Peter and John were released from prison in Acts 4, they gathered with the church to pray for more boldness, and for the Lord to work signs and wonders. Prayer was the church's means of receiving strength and guidance from the Lord. They depended on intimate communion with the One in whom they had put their trust.

Sadly, our churches aren't typically characterized by devotion to prayer. Could it be that we have lost sight of our absolute dependence on God? Have we lost the urgency of our mission and the sense that if God does not work through us, we will not be able to do what we have been called to do? Prayer is exactly this type of declaration. A church that is devoted to prayer is a church that knows God's mission is the most important pursuit on earth. It is a church that knows it cannot succeed without God. May this type of devotion to prayer define the attitude of our churches.

5. *Explain why prayer is essential to the life and mission of the church. What would a devotion to prayer look like in the life of your church?*

More Than Individuals

The early church was made up of those who embraced the gospel. God's Spirit had been poured out on them and their sins had been forgiven. These people had been saved from a "crooked generation" (Acts 2:40). This is exactly what the church has been in all ages. The church consists of those who have been called out of their spiritual darkness and have responded to the good news that Jesus Christ died to remove the separation of sin and rose from the grave to demonstrate that He is the true King of the world. In every generation, God takes those He is redeeming and joins them together in the church.

Individualism is widely celebrated in our culture. We like to think of ourselves as self-sufficient and independent, able to "make it on our own." Sadly, many Christians have adopted this individualistic mindset. Nobody is going to tell us how to spend our time or our money or tell us what to think. Sound familiar? If so, then we need to look long and hard at the early church's life together.

Notice what the first Christian converts in Acts 2 did not do. They did not simply make a profession of faith and then seek to live the Christian life on their own. No, these early converts were baptized as a sign of their identification with Jesus Christ and His church. Actually, to identify with Jesus Christ is to identify with the church, His beloved bride. Jesus Himself said: "By this all people will know that you are my disciples, if you have love for another" (John 13:35). One crucial aspect of submitting to Jesus is committing to the ministry of His church. We are no longer isolated individuals, but members of Christ's body.

6. *Read 1 Corinthians 12. How should Paul's analogy of the church as a body affect the way we think about the church?*

7. *Does the life of your church look anything like the body that Paul described in 1 Corinthians 12? How so? If not, why do you think this is?*

What Are We Missing?

Reading the book of Acts can almost be depressing because we are forced to recognize deficiencies in our churches. On the one hand, this is healthy. We should be challenged by the vitality of the early church. But on the other hand, we need to be careful not to simply imitate what we see in Acts. God gave a mission to the church, and it worked out in a specific way in the life of the early church. We have the same mission, but God may want to do something unique in our churches. Rather than trying to reproduce the tongues of fire, the powerful sermon, and the mass conversion we find in Acts 2, we should be looking for God to fulfill His purposes through our churches in whatever ways He sees fit. Read through the following description of life in the early church, then take some time to consider how some of the characteristics of the early church might play out in your unique setting.

A Generous Community

Members of the early church had such a concern for their brothers and sisters in Christ that they were willing to sell their own possessions to meet a physical need. The Scriptures say that they had "all things in common" (Acts 2:44; see also 4:32). In other words, these Christians voluntarily gave of what they had for the welfare of fellow believers. Likewise, Paul described a time when the churches in Macedonia joyfully gave even in the midst of "extreme poverty" (2 Cor. 8:2). He even said, "they gave according to their means, as I can testify, and beyond their means, of their own accord, begging us earnestly for the favor of taking part in the relief of the saints" (vv. 3–4). Such generosity is the fruit of transformed hearts.

A Holy Community

The early church was a community set apart for God's purposes. Even the outside world took notice of what was happening. Luke says that "awe came upon every soul" (Acts 2:43). This group of believers was noticeably different from the outside world. Their obedience and God's presence among them caused them to stand out, so that they had favor with the unbelievers around them (2:47).

A Fearless Community

Not everyone was happy about the Holy Spirit's work in the early church. Suffering was a very real part of following Jesus in the first century, and the same holds true today. Christians around the world are often under physical threat for confessing Jesus Christ, while our own culture continues to grow increasingly intolerant of the gospel message. Paul promised: "all who desire to live a godly life in Christ Jesus will be persecuted" (2 Tim. 3:12). The early church boldly proclaimed the truth of the gospel and fearlessly reached out to the hurting world around them. Because of this, they often encountered persecution and even martyrdom.

A Multiplying Community

There's no denying that the growth of the early church was remarkable. What began as a small band of fledgling disciples multiplied supernaturally into a large movement consisting of believers in Jerusalem, Judea, Samaria, and eventually to the ends of the earth (Acts 1:8). Churches were planted as the apostles and other believers took the gospel all over the known world. All of this was clearly the Lord's work: "*the Lord added* to their number day by day those who were being saved" (Acts 2:47).

In a providential twist, it was often the persecution of the church that resulted in its growth. As believers were scattered, they took the gospel with them (Acts 8:1). Instead of retreating into silence, they prayed for boldness when they came under scrutiny from the authorities (Acts 4:23–31). We are reminded that the Lord's plan for growing His church turns the world's wisdom on its head.

8. *What do you find most compelling about the way the book of Acts describes the life of the early church?*

9. *Does your church possess these compelling characteristics? If so, briefly describe them and thank God for them. If not, why do you think these characteristics are lacking?*

The Church in the Modern World

Read through almost any letter in the New Testament, and you'll quickly see that the early Christian churches were anything but perfect. In fact, many of these letters were written to address specific sins or false teachings. For example, the Galatian Christians were in danger of distorting the gospel (Gal. 1:6), while the church at Corinth was tolerating gross sexual sin (1 Cor. 5:1). Or take an example from the early Christian congregation in Acts: one part of the church felt that their widows were being neglected in comparison with another part of the church (Acts 6:1). Similar complaints threaten to divide many of our own churches today. Our experience may be closer to the early Christians than we think.

In this session we have highlighted many of the positive characteristics about life in the early church, and Acts certainly gives us much to imitate in the example they set. God's Spirit worked in extraordinary ways in order to empower the church for its mission. However, we have misunderstood the early church if we feel that we cannot relate to the early church's experience. This group of believers did not live in some spiritual fantasyland untouched by sin and weakness. In fact, the point of their example is not primarily to make us dwell on their strengths, but rather to make us marvel at God's strength. His Spirit caused the message of Christ to bear fruit as it was taken to city after city.

The church must continue to exalt Jesus Christ in our own day by the power of the Spirit. We shouldn't expect to experience another Day of Pentecost, or to see precisely the same signs and wonders that the apostles performed, but we should continue to pray that the Holy Spirit will transform the way we live and give us boldness to proclaim the good news to the people around us. The same God who multiplied the early church works through the church today. And the same Spirit who lived in the midst of the Christians in the first century lives within the church of the twenty-first century. It is our responsibility to bring that same message of healing and salvation to our modern world through the power and guidance of the Holy Spirit.

10. *What do you think the Holy Spirit would want your church to do in an effort to fulfill the church's mission in your unique setting? If you don't have an answer for this, make it a priority to pray and seek the Spirit's guidance on this issue.*

11. *Spend some time in prayer. Ask God to guide and empower your church for the mission He has given you. Pray that the church today would be everything that God designed it to be.*

Watch the video for this session at multiplymovement.com.

5: Good News for All Nations

Is Jesus your *personal* Savior? That's a common phrase in the Christian world. Jesus should be your personal Savior. But make sure He is much more than that. Jesus absolutely saves individuals in a personal way. If your broken relationship with God has been restored, it's because Jesus sacrificed Himself for your sin and God's grace has renewed your heart. This happens to individuals—no one is saved because she has Christian parents, attends a church service, or lives in a "Christian nation."

But your relationship with God should not be characterized by individualism. God worked in your individual heart to give you new life, but salvation is not about your making it to heaven as an individual. Jesus saves us as individuals to place us within a body—the church. In reality, Jesus is the Savior *of the church*. He died to create a people who together love and worship Him and fulfill His purposes in the world.

This means that the gospel is not only good news *for me*, it is good news *for everyone*. Jesus is the Savior of the world (John 11:51–52; 1 John 2:2). With Adam and Eve, the whole world fell into sin. With Jesus, the whole world can be redeemed, restored, saved, made new (Rom. 5:18). God's plan of redemption has always been global in scope. There is not a single tribe, tongue, or nation on the planet that will not be affected by the gospel of Jesus Christ (Rev. 5:9). The good news is for all nations (Luke 2:10).

God's Plan for the Nations

Spreading the gospel to the ends of the earth was not a new plan implemented by Jesus and His disciples. From the very beginning, God's intention was to restore every aspect of the world He created. His plan of salvation is not for the Jews only, but also the Gentiles (a broad term that simply means "non-Jews").

The Old Testament pointed ahead to a day when all people, both Jew and Gentile, would come to the one true God. God promised Abraham that in him *all the nations* of the earth would be blessed (Gen. 18:18). Similarly, the psalmist exclaimed, "Let the peoples praise you, O God; let *all the peoples* praise you!" (Ps. 67:5). God told Isaiah: "I will make you a light for the nations, that my salvation may reach to the end of the earth" (Is. 49:6). God's heart has always extended to every nation on earth.

When Jesus came as the Messiah, He demonstrated the world-wide scope of His mission. Even though His initial focus was to go to the "lost sheep of … Israel" (Matt. 15:24), He always had a larger goal in mind. The Jews tended to focus on their national heritage and to look down on the Gentiles. They particularly disliked a group called the Samaritans. Yet Jesus had a loving discussion with a Samaritan woman in John 4 and demonstrated His heart for those outside of the people of Israel. Similarly, Jesus healed the demon-oppressed daughter of a Canaanite woman (Matt. 15:28). Jesus's goal was "to seek and to save the lost" (Luke 19:10), including the wealthy and the poor, the accepted and the outcast, the Jew and the Gentile. Luke's gospel especially highlights this theme, where God's grace reaches even the least likely.

The Great Commission (Matt. 28:18–20) proves that Jesus wants all people to know Him. Both then and now He works through His disciples by His Spirit to accomplish this very purpose.

1. *How should God's heart as revealed in the Old Testament and in Jesus's ministry affect the way we think about and relate to those people who seem "unreachable"?*

A Jewish Messiah for All People

After He rose from the grave, Jesus announced to His disciples that the Holy Spirit would empower them so that they could be His witnesses "in Jerusalem and in all Judea and Samaria, and to the end of the earth" (Acts 1:8). The rest of the book of Acts explains how this played out, beginning with the growth of the church in Jerusalem

(Acts 2) and ending with Paul's proclamation of the gospel from prison in Rome (Acts 28).

Acts 10 records an especially significant moment in the history of the church. God directly sent Peter (who, like the rest of the disciples, was a Jew) to bring the gospel to Cornelius (a Gentile) and his household. At this point in history, the Jews avoided close contact with the Gentiles. Yet God gave Peter a vision to show him that the gospel was for all the nations. As Peter told this household of Gentiles about the new life that God offers through Jesus Christ, they believed, and God testified to the validity of their belief by sending the Holy Spirit upon them.

As the gospel continued to take root in the non-Jewish world, a question emerged: Did these Gentiles need to become Jews before they could become Christians? Remember that God's plan of redemption had been firmly rooted in the people of Israel from the time that God chose to bless Abraham. Jesus was a Jew, and the concept of the Messiah was Jewish to the core. Some believed that while the Gentiles were invited to share in the life of the Jewish Messiah, they could only do so by taking on a distinctly Jewish identity.

The issue came to a head in Acts 15, when the leaders of the church gathered in Jerusalem to decide how these Gentile converts should be handled. Should they submit to the Law of Moses? Did they need to be circumcised and offer sacrifices? James offered this solution:

> We should not trouble those of the Gentiles who
> turn to God, but should write to them to abstain
> from the things polluted by idols, and from sexual

immorality, and from what has been strangled, and from blood. (Acts 15:19–20)

Basically, they decided that being a Christian is not the same thing as being a Jew. This was a turning point in the spread of the gospel. While Christianity will always have Jewish roots, it is not bound to a particular ethnicity. The gospel is good news for all nations.

2. *Read Acts 15. How is the global aspect of God's plan of redemption demonstrated in this passage?*

An Apostle to the Gentiles

When God chose Paul to be an apostle, He specifically called him to reach the Gentiles. The second half of Acts focuses on Paul's ministry and follows his missionary journeys across the vast Roman Empire. In most church circles today, we tend to think of Paul mainly as a theologian. We explore his letters as we look for answers to deep theological questions. But most likely, Paul would have thought of himself primarily as a missionary.

Paul said that he received his apostleship "to bring about the obedience of faith for the sake of his name among all the nations" (Rom. 1:5). His ambition was to share the good news in areas that had not yet heard about what Jesus had done (Rom. 15:20). And when people responded and began to meet together as Christians, he urged them to walk in obedience.

Paul had some important things to say about the Jew/Gentile question. He argued that faith in Jesus Christ was all that was necessary to become part of God's people. It's not about fulfilling the Jewish law or identifying with a certain ethnicity—all people have sinned (Rom. 3:23), therefore all people need God and His salvation. Jesus's life, death, and resurrection are the only bases for sinners to be reconciled to a holy God, regardless of their ethnicity or background. No other work or ceremony is necessary. To add to this firm foundation is to pervert the gospel (Gal. 1:8). Paul could not have been more clear on this important issue:

> There is neither Jew nor Greek, there is neither slave nor free, there is no male and female, for you are all one in Christ Jesus. And if you are Christ's, then you are Abraham's offspring, heirs according to promise. (Gal. 3:28–29)

3. *Take a minute to meditate on Galatians 3:28–29. Why do you think Paul made such a big deal about the relationship between Jews and Gentiles?*

The Missionary Church

Proclaiming the gospel to a lost world cannot be just another activity to add to the church's crowded agenda. It must be central to who we are. It forms our identity. Being a follower of Christ means being a part of this mission. The gospel message was never intended to be a private matter. As Jesus told His disciples, "A city set on a hill cannot be hidden" (Matt. 5:14). The light was intended to invade the darkness. The entire New Testament is about Christ's redeeming the world and calling every nation on earth to praise Him for this.

When Jesus called the twelve disciples to follow Him, He promised to make them "fishers of men" (Matt. 4:19; Mark 1:17). These disciples, some of them former fishermen, would now "fish" by telling people what they had heard and seen in Christ's ministry, death, and resurrection. Their goal was to be intentionally seeking new followers of Christ. Though Jesus certainly spoke about how we are to live our lives, His instructions were far more than an ethical code to be admired. He was preparing His followers to engage in the battle for souls.

In our modern world, it is increasingly popular to keep your faith to yourself, to not "push your beliefs on others." But according to Jesus's commands, our faith is anything but private. He tells us to proclaim His message everywhere and make disciples of all nations (Matt. 28:18–20). These are our marching orders, regardless of whether or not the world approves.

Every aspect of our world has been stained by sin and death. From the very beginning, God has had one plan of redemption, a plan that reached its culmination in the person of Jesus Christ. The people around us may not realize that they are lost and broken (though they often do), but the world is in desperate need of redemption. God is working to set this broken world to rights. As we will see in the next session, this will not be fully accomplished until the story ends. But He has given His church the task of sharing His good news and bringing healing to that which is broken.

4. *What does it mean to be a "fisher of men"?*

5. *Is there anything about your life that would identify you as a "fisher of men"? If so, what? If not, what can you do to grow in this area?*

We all have a responsibility to take part in this mission, but we will all play different roles. Some of us will be sharing the gospel in some remote jungle or deep within Muslim territory. Others will be sharing the gospel locally while training others to go to the less-reached areas. Those who feel called to spread the gospel locally should still pray diligently and give sacrificially for those who leave.

We all have to be involved. Carrying the good news into every corner of the world is the mission that Jesus left for us. Missions cannot simply be a department of your church. It should be a vital consideration in everything your church does. A church that does not care about reaching the nations is not a church in the New Testament sense. It's our identity. It cannot be neglected without compromising who we are and dishonoring the One we claim to serve.

6. *How would you describe your church's attitude toward and participation in spreading the gospel to all nations? How might you encourage your church to work toward this end?*

7. *What is your own involvement with missions? Are you at all involved in going, sending, training, supplying, praying, etc.? What changes might you need to make to this area of your life?*

The Multicultural Community of the Redeemed

The book of Revelation assures us that God's purpose to save people from "every tribe and language and people and nation" (Rev. 5:9) *will* succeed. Let there be no confusion: God's mission cannot fail!

While aspects of Revelation can be confusing for all of us at times, it clearly teaches that God will redeem a people from all parts of the earth through the death of His Son, Jesus Christ. It seems the apostle John (the author of Revelation) was overwhelmed as he wrote:

> After this I looked, and behold, a great multitude
> that no one could number, from every nation,
> from all tribes and peoples and languages, standing
> before the throne and before the Lamb, clothed in
> white robes, with palm branches in their hands, and
> crying out with a loud voice, "Salvation belongs to
> our God who sits on the throne, and to the Lamb!"
> (Rev. 7:9–10)

This picture of worship in the book of Revelation should give us confidence in our great God. All authority belongs to Him, and His plans always succeed. Therefore, we should have confidence as we reach out to the world around us. Because the Holy Spirit empowers us, we can be certain that our effort to make disciples of all nations is not futile. With God on our side, victory is assured. If God is for us, who can be against us (Rom. 8:31)? Even when we are rejected and endure suffering for our witness, God is completely in control. The power of the gospel will ultimately prevail. So, pray, go, share, and rejoice in the Lord Jesus Christ.

8. *How does this picture of a multiethnic multitude worshipping God at the end of history affect the way you think about our task of reaching out to the nations?*

9. *Spend some time in prayer. Ask God to give you a burning desire to see the good news of Jesus Christ embraced in every corner of the world. Ask Him to show you what part He wants you to play in seeing His name spread around the world.*

   Watch the video for this session at multiplymovement.com.

6: The End of the Story

The more we think about the end, the stronger and more effective we will be as Christians. It keeps us focused on the goal. It reminds us that God is not finished working and that everything will be accomplished in God's perfect timing.

How often do you meditate on the way the world will end?

With this session, we come to the end of the biblical storyline. As we have seen, God's good world fell under the power of the curse after Adam and Eve rejected the reign of their King. The Bible recounts God's plan of redemption as it plays out in the promises to Abraham, the exodus of Israel, the Law of Moses, and the royal throne of David. This plan of redemption reaches its culmination in the life, death, and resurrection of Jesus and carries into the life of the church as Jesus sends the Holy Spirit to empower His people to continue God's mission.

In essence, the story of the Bible follows God's actions as He works out His plan to reverse the effects of the fall. God created human beings in His own image and placed them in the midst of His good world to shape it and lovingly rule over it on His behalf. But from the moment Adam and Eve rebelled against God, this world has been under the curse, stained by sin and death. As Paul put it, the entire creation is groaning to be set free from its bondage to corruption (Rom. 8:19–22). God's comprehensive plan of redemption is to reverse everything that sin has done to corrupt this world. The Bible begins with the statement that "In the beginning, God created the heavens and the earth" and ends with God's declaration: "Behold, I am making all things new" (Rev. 21:5).

The Beginning of the End

We can't talk about the end without talking about Jesus. Our final salvation is coming at the end of history when Jesus returns. But that salvation has already been purchased and secured. Jesus assured us of this when He announced from the cross: "It is finished" (John 19:30). Whatever will take place in the future, our hope is secured in the reality that Jesus has acted decisively in history and restored our broken relationship with God. Jesus's life, death, and resurrection were not just *a part* of the story of redemption; they were the climax. This was where Eve's descendant crushed the head of the Enemy (Gen. 3:15).

Because of what Jesus has done on our behalf, history is moving toward a glorious end. Just as history changed when Jesus came to earth, everything will be changed again when He returns (an event we refer to as "the Second Coming"). The author of Hebrews explained the significance of both of Jesus's appearances on earth:

> He has appeared once for all at the end of the ages
> to put away sin by the sacrifice of himself. And just
> as it is appointed for man to die once, and after that
> comes judgment, so Christ, having been offered
> once to bear the sins of many, will appear a second
> time, not to deal with sin but to save those who are
> eagerly waiting for him. (Heb. 9:26–28)

Jesus appeared the first time to sacrifice Himself and secure our salvation, and He will appear again to bring that salvation to fruition. This is the future that history is moving toward. This is how the world will end.

Christians tend to disagree about many points of theology, especially when it comes to future events. Theological camps have formed around differing views of how the end times will unfold. Much of the disagreement centers on the precise timeline of end-times prophecies. Some of these Old and New Testament prophecies are notoriously difficult to interpret. Because some of these concepts are tough and have at times caused division, many choose to avoid the topic altogether—as if the end of the world isn't really that big of a deal. But Jesus often spoke about the end. In fact, holding on to the promise of the end can help to carry us through difficult situations today. As Christians, peace comes from knowing our pain will end. Joy results from our confidence that Jesus is returning to make all things new.

It would be wrong for us to ignore end-times events, but there are some issues that are too complex to sort out here. We will focus on the big picture and the concepts that God clearly wants us to recognize in these prophecies.

1. *Have you done much studying or thinking on how and when the world will end? If so, what has been your impression of the end times? If not, why do you think you haven't approached this issue in the past?*

What We've All Been Longing For

Throughout history, humanity has not been able to shake the feeling that there is something wrong with the world. People have tried to blame God, political leaders, religions, and just about everyone and everything else for the disappointment we feel about the state of the world. We see the problem in the crimes we hear about on the news, and also in the frustrations and injustices we experience in our daily lives. This problem even permeates the very thoughts that pass through our minds. There is something fundamentally wrong with the world, and it pervades every aspect of our existence.

As Christians, we see some of the effects of the fall reversed in our lives. The gospel has freed us from bondage to sin (Rom. 6), and the Spirit of God enables us to follow Jesus in ways that non-Christians cannot (Rom. 8 and Gal. 5). But we also experience an added struggle—Paul promised that everyone who desires to live a godly life will experience persecution (2 Tim. 3:12). We experience the joy of the Lord, but life in a fallen world is difficult and often disappointing.

We are called to faithfully follow Jesus in the midst of this sin-stained world, but we also have the sweet promise that it won't be like this forever. Jesus will return, and the world will be set to rights. Whereas we now experience injustice, God will bring justice. Where there is division, God will bring peace. Where there is sin, God will bring righteousness. This is the promise that carries us along when we feel as though this world is too broken to be fixed or that we are too weak to endure much longer.

2. *Read Romans 8:18–25. How does this promise affect your view of the world?*

The Return of the King

The most important thing that we should understand about the future is that Jesus is coming back. When He returned to His Father, He left the church to carry on His mission and sent the Holy Spirit to empower us for the task. But Jesus is not done with this world. He will return, and when He does, He will rule over a perfect, peaceful, re-created earth.

Read the first chapter of Revelation and you will quickly see that Jesus's second coming will be much different from His first. The meek Servant, once ridiculed and spat upon, is shown to be the Ruler of the universe and worthy to be feared. At His return, Jesus will bring final salvation to His people, restore justice to the earth, and destroy all of God's enemies. The book of Revelation records fierce warfare and portrays Jesus as a conquering King, boldly reclaiming the world that rightfully belongs to Him (Rev. 19). As weak as the church has seemed at some points in history, as persecuted and defeated as we sometimes feel, this is what lies in our future.

God's plan of redemption has never been contingent. There has never been any doubt about the way history will end. This is God's world; He created it; He vowed to reclaim it; He died to purchase His people, and finally, when the time arrives, He will come and take this world by force. Paul illustrated the reality of this last day powerfully:

> Therefore [because of Jesus's obedience and sacrifice] God has highly exalted him and bestowed on him the name that is above every name, so that at the name of Jesus every knee should bow, in heaven and on earth and under the earth, and every tongue confess that Jesus Christ is Lord, to the glory of God the Father. (Phil. 2:9–11)

No matter how much opposition we face, the day will come when everyone will see Jesus for who He truly is. His reign will finally be realized on earth in the same way that it has always been realized in heaven.

3. *Read Revelation 1. Based on this description of Jesus, how will Jesus in His second coming be different from in His first coming?*

The New Heavens and New Earth

Turn to the last pages of the Bible and you will find a beautiful picture of creation restored. The first chapters of Genesis and the last chapters of Revelation function as bookends to God's plan of redemption. In Genesis, God created all things and called them "good" (Gen. 1–2). People were created to have fellowship with God and to reflect His glory as a ruling steward of creation. In similar fashion, the Bible ends with a picture of a new creation: "Then I saw a new heaven and a new earth" (Rev. 21:1). This new creation was anticipated in the Old Testament, so it is no accident that Revelation describes the new creation using imagery from both the garden in Eden and the temple in Jerusalem. These locations, the garden and the temple, were God's meeting places with humanity. The leaves of the tree of life will now bring healing, and the river of the water of life will flow from God's throne (22:1–2). There is also a new Jerusalem; only this holy city has no need for a temple building, because "its temple is the Lord God the Almighty and the Lamb" (21:22).

Everything about the old creation that has been marred by sin and death is no more, for God has made all things new. The new creation will be so full of joy that it seems difficult to fathom. But the best news about this new creation, this eternal paradise, is not that the flowers will be more beautiful or the grass will be greener, or even that our bodies will be free from disease (as great as those things will be); rather, the greatest feature of the new creation is that we will have perfect communion with God. Listen to how John put it: "Behold, the dwelling place of God is with man. He will dwell with them, and they will be His people, and God himself will be with them as their God" (21:3). This statement echoes the covenants that God made with His people from the very beginning, and it points toward the reality that we are all longing for. Imagine what it will be like to physically see our Holy God dwelling with us.

This fellowship with God extends far beyond one man (as in the case of Abraham) or one nation (as in the case of Israel). We read of people from "every tribe and language and people and nation" (5:9) who will be worshipping at Jesus's throne. The command that Jesus gave in the Great Commission to make disciples of all nations will finally be fulfilled. God's purposes for this world will finally be accomplished. Redemption will be completed.

4. *Read Revelation 21–22. As you read this beautiful description of the New Creation, don't get caught up in trying to interpret every detail. Instead, try to picture and feel the beauty and peace of the scene that awaits us. What stands out to you most from reading this account?*

5. *Based on what you read in Revelation 21–22 and what you read and discussed in the session on creation, how will God's new creation reflect the reality of God's initial creation before the fall? How will it be better?*

A Day of Judgment

There is also a horrifying flip side to this glorious consummation in Revelation. Everlasting judgment awaits those who have rejected God and opposed His people. Sin will be seen for what it is—not an inconsequential part of life, but a serious affront to God. Those who do evil will be kept out of the glorious city. Christ will judge people according to what they have done (22:12), and only those who are united to Jesus will be allowed to enter. The rest will be cast into the lake of fire (Rev. 20:11–15).

This should cause us to literally tremble as we think of those who have not submitted to Jesus as Lord (see Rom. 9:1–3). Our mission to those who are lost could not be more urgent. The unreached people groups across the globe and our next-door neighbors need to hear the only message that can save them.

What about you? Do you understand the extent to which sin stains your life and separates you from the Holy God of the universe? Do you see your rebellion for what it is? Have you embraced the sacrifice that Jesus made to remove your sin and restore your relationship with God? Or are you under the illusion that your own moral effort will grant you access to God's everlasting rest? Hear Jesus's words: "To the thirsty I will give from the spring of the water of life without payment" (21:6). Come, believe, and drink freely.

6. *How should the promise of judgment at Jesus's return affect the way we think about and interact with the non-Christians in our lives?*

7. *Is there anyone in your life whom you need to be more purposeful in reaching out to? If so, spend some time asking the Holy Spirit to give you confidence and wisdom in reaching out to this person with the gospel.*

Living with the End in View

The message of Revelation has huge implications for the way we live our lives today. It's not just about what will happen in the future. Just as God's actions in the past should affect the way we live today, so God's actions in the future should shape everything we do now. One of the strongest features of the book of Revelation is its encouragement to remain faithful in the midst of seemingly hopeless circumstances.

When the apostle John wrote Revelation, he was in exile on the isle of Patmos. He was banished there because he refused to stop preaching the gospel (Rev. 1:9). As he waited in exile, God gave John a glimpse of the world as it really is, and as it really will be in the future. Although the then-dominant Roman Empire seemed to be in control of the known world, John received a different picture of reality—he saw the world as God sees it. The book of Revelation essentially conveys this message to seven churches during the first century AD, and by extension, to all Christians.

The message to the seven churches in Revelation, and to us today, is that we cannot let go of our commitment to Jesus Christ. Although we may face opposition and suffering, Jesus is reigning over every earthly authority. The judgment that is coming upon those who reject Christ is terrible, but believers should long for Christ's return, since their ultimate destination is a new creation. God's purposes will ultimately succeed, and the good news will be proclaimed and believed in every part of the earth. Revelation calls those who don't follow Jesus to repent and receive the salvation Jesus offers before it is too late. It also calls those who are followers of Jesus to stand strong until the end.

Peter warned us that in the last days, people will mock us for believing that Jesus will return: "Where is the promise of his coming? For ever since the fathers fell asleep, all things are continuing as they were from the beginning of creation" (2 Pet. 3:4). In other words, "We haven't seen Him do anything to punish the wicked, so why should we believe that there will be a day of judgment?" Peter's answer offers us great hope:

> But do not overlook this one fact, beloved, that with the Lord one day is as a thousand years, and a thousand years as one day. The Lord is not slow to fulfill his promise as some count slowness, but is patient toward you, not wishing that any should perish, but that all should reach repentance. But the day of the Lord will come like a thief, and then the heavens will pass away with a roar, and the heavenly bodies will be burned up and dissolved, and the earth and the works that are done on it will be exposed.
>
> Since all these things are thus to be dissolved, what sort of people ought you to be in lives of holiness and godliness, waiting for and hastening the coming of the day of God, because of which the heavens will be set on fire and dissolved, and the heavenly bodies will melt as they burn! But according to his promise we are waiting for new heavens and a new earth in which righteousness dwells.
>
> Therefore, beloved, since you are waiting for these, be diligent to be found by him without spot or blemish, and at peace. (2 Pet. 3:8–14)

Make no mistake, Jesus is returning. He is patiently waiting for the men and women He created to repent, but He will not wait forever. The day will come when this world that He created will be purified by fire, just as the world was purified by a flood in Noah's day. The reality of judgment and the promise of the new heavens and new earth should motivate us to remain faithful to Jesus now. We do not need to doubt that God's plan of redemption will come to completion, but the end toward which history is headed should set our agenda for today.

8. *How should the end of the story affect the way we live today? Be as specific to your own situation as possible.*

Why We Make Disciples

The Bible ends with these words: "He who testifies to these things says, 'Surely I am coming soon.' Amen. Come, Lord Jesus! The grace of the Lord Jesus be with all. Amen" (Rev. 22:20–21). Our God-given task is to reach into every corner of creation and make disciples of all nations. Jesus gave us this command when He left, and He is coming again soon.

This life is about Jesus and His glory. Our mission is about God and His plan of redemption. We have seen God's story of redemption unfold from the moment Adam and Eve ate the forbidden fruit until the early church spread the good news about Jesus around the known world. The church also has a two-thousand-year history of continuing the mission of making disciples and spreading the gospel around the world (though we have not always done this perfectly). And in this session, we have seen where the story will end.

We can follow the storyline from beginning to end, yet there is one gap that still remains in the story, and that is the part that we are called to play. The end of the story has been written, but we still have a responsibility to faithfully play our part. The hope and healing of the gospel still needs to reach people all around the world *today*. This moment has been entrusted to us by God. Making disciples has always been the calling of the church, and it is our responsibility to be devoted to that end.

Jesus said,

> All authority in heaven and on earth has been given to me. Go therefore and make disciples of all nations, baptizing them in the name of the Father and of the Son and of the Holy Spirit, teaching them to observe all that I have commanded you. And behold, I am with you always, to the end of the age. (Matt. 28:18–20)

The King has full authority, and He has given us this command. He will be with us always, even to the end of the age. We don't know exactly when the end will come, but we know that making disciples is what we need to be doing. Let us pray that when Jesus returns, He will find us faithfully pursuing His mission with the skills, relationships, and resources that He has entrusted to us.

9. *Spend some time in prayer. Thank God that Jesus will return to set the world to rights and that His plan of redemption will be completed. Ask God to affect your heart with the reality of what the future holds. Ask Him to guide you and empower you to live as a faithful disciple maker at this moment in history.*

 Watch the video for this session at multiplymovement.com.

Where Do We Go from Here?

Now that you have finished *Multiply*, we want to be clear that you're not done. The call to make disciples is not about getting through a book, completing a set number of sessions, or growing from Point A to Point B. The mission we have been given claims every aspect of our lives from now until the day we die or Christ returns. Completing this material is a milestone, but it is not the end.

So where do we go from here?

First, understand that reading about the Bible is not a substitute for actually reading the Bible. We trust that what we have written here has given you some helpful tools and perspective on what the Bible is and how to study it carefully and obediently. But if you stop here, then it has all been a huge waste of time. The point is that you go on from here to spend a lifetime of reading God's Word and doing what it says.

It is helpful to read and talk about the Bible, but remember that there is something unique about actually reading the Bible directly.

God's Word is actually *living* and *active* (Heb. 4:12). It gets inside of you; it transforms you from within. We should talk about God's truth often. But we can't talk about God's Word if we are not reading it regularly. We need to be saturating ourselves in Scripture so that it naturally comes out in every area of our lives.

Reading the Bible is simple, but if you discipline yourself to make it a regular part of your life, it will transform you in more ways than you can imagine. Obviously you will want to read as much of the Bible as you can, but don't let your ambition become a roadblock. Some people have the time and ability to read larger sections of Scripture than others. Start with an attainable goal, and if you find that you are able to read more than you planned, that's great. All of the Bible is important, but it's not about how much you can read in a single sitting. It's about allowing God to speak to you through His Word and responding in obedience and faith.

With each section of Scripture you read ask yourself two questions:

1. What is God saying in this passage?
2. How am I going to respond?

Be sure to use the skills you learned in Part III about studying the Bible.

Second, don't let this be the end of your disciple making. If you have just finished walking someone through this material, then begin reading through books of the Bible with that person. Choose a passage of Scripture that you will read through, then get together and talk about what you learned. You're going to find plenty of things in each passage that you don't understand fully. That's okay. It's not about knowing everything. There are answers out there, but being a disciple maker is not about knowing all of the answers. It's about being committed to following Jesus and taking seriously His command to help other people follow Him more fully.

As you meet with the person you are discipling, don't worry about overpreparing. Study the passage on your own, then get together and share what stood out to each of you. What did you learn? What does God seem to be saying? What questions do you have? How should these truths be applied to your life? How can you help each other faithfully follow Jesus in light of this passage of Scripture?

Discussing Scripture in this way is not simply a means of becoming more knowledgeable, it is a way of building a relationship that is focused on God and saturated in His Word. God's Word will constantly challenge and transform you.

Finally, we encourage you to find someone else to take through *Multiply*. If you have been walking someone through this material, keep reading the Bible with that person and find someone else to begin this process with. If you have just been guided through the material by someone else, then take what you have learned and walk someone else through it.

Paul showed the multiplying effect of disciple making when he told Timothy: "What you have heard from me in the presence of many witnesses entrust to faithful men who will be able to teach others also" (2 Tim. 2:2). The process never ends. This is how the church grows and continues to build itself up. This is the mission that Jesus left for us, and it is what we want to be found doing when He returns.

For your church.
For your small group.
For you.